Shrinking Fields:
Cropland Loss in a World
of Eight Billion

GARY GARDNER

Jane A. Peterson, *Editor*

WORLDWATCH PAPER 131
July 1996

FINANCIAL SUPPORT is provided by Carolyn Foundation, the Nathan Cummings Foundation, the Geraldine R. Dodge Foundation, the Energy Foundation, The Ford Foundation, the George Gund Foundation, The William and Flora Hewlett Foundation, W. Alton Jones Foundation, John D. and Catherine T. MacArthur Foundation, Andrew W. Mellon Foundation, The Curtis and Edith Munson Foundation, Edward John Noble Foundation, The Pew Charitable Trusts, Lynn R. and Karl E. Prickett Fund, Rockefeller Brothers Fund, Rockefeller Financial Services, Surdna Foundation, Turner Foundation, U.N. Population Fund, Wallace Genetic Foundation, Wallace Global Fund, Weeden Foundation, and the Winslow Foundation.

PUBLICATIONS of the Institute include the annual *State of the World*, which is now published in 27 languages; *Vital Signs*, an annual compendium of global trends that are shaping our future; the *Environmental Alert* book series; *World Watch* magazine; and the Worldwatch Papers. For more information on Worldwatch publications, write: Worldwatch Institute, 1776 Massachusetts Ave., NW, Washington, DC 20036; or fax 202-296-7365; or see back pages.

THE WORLDWATCH PAPERS provide in-depth, quantitative and qualitative analysis of the major issues affecting prospects for a sustainable society. The Papers are written by members of the Worldwatch Institute research staff and reviewed by experts in the field. Published in five languages, they have been used as concise and authoritative references by governments, nongovernmental organizations, and educational institutions worldwide. For a partial list of available Papers, see back pages.

DATA from all graphs and tables contained in this Paper are available on 3 1/2" Macintosh or IBM-compatible computer disks. The disks also include data from the *State of the World* series, *Vital Signs*, *Environmental Alert* book series, Worldwatch Papers, and *World Watch* magazine. Each yearly subscription includes a mid-year update, and *Vital Signs* and *State of the World* as they are published. The disk is formatted for Lotus 1-2-3, and can be used with Quattro Pro, Excel, SuperCalc, and many other spreadsheets. To order, see back pages.

Table of Contents

Introduction 5

Trends: From Surplus to Scarcity 8

Expanding Cities 12

Evaporating Irrigated Land 19

Degrading Our Future 25

Changing Tastes 31

A Land-Scarce World 35

Land for the Next Generation 41

Notes 48

Tables and Figures

Table 1: *Loss of Arable Land in China, 1987–92* 15

Table 2: *Share of Agricultural Land with Degraded Soils* 27

Table 3: *Selected Examples of Soil Degradation* 28

Figure 1: *World Grain Harvested Area, 1950–96* 9

Figure 2: *World Grain Harvested Area Per Person, 1950–96* 10

Figure 3: *World Soybean Harvested Area, 1950–95* 33

Figure 4: *World Grain Harvested Area Per Person, 1950–2030* 37

For one-time academic use of this material, please contact Customer Service, Copyright Clearance Center, at (508) 750-8400 (phone), or (508) 750-4744 (fax), or write to CCC, 222 Rosewood Drive, Danvers, MA 01923. Nonacademic users, please call the Worldwatch Institute's Communication Department at (202) 452-1992, x520, or fax your request to (202) 296-7365.

ACKNOWLEDGMENTS: I am grateful to Norm Berg, Charles Beretz, Pierre Crosson, Sally Bolger, and Sandra Postel, and to my colleagues Lester Brown, Christopher Flavin, and Jennifer Mitchell for helpful comments on early drafts of this paper. Jennifer also provided exceptionally thorough and rapid assistance with research and, along with colleagues Hal Kane and Michael Renner, helped me to clarify key points. Lori Ann Baldwin and Laura Malinowski were always willing and able to track down obscure books and journals. Finally, Worldwatch colleagues Jennifer Seher, Jim Perry, and Denise Byers Thomma, and our editor, Jane Peterson, supportively and patiently navigated the turbid waters of the production process. To all, a heartfelt thank you.

GARY GARDNER is a Research Associate at the Worldwatch Institute, where he writes on agriculture, water, and international economics. Since joining the Institute in 1994, he has written a chapter in *State of the World 1996*, and contributed to *Vital Signs 1995* and *World Watch* magazine. He will be one of the Institute's representatives at the World Food Summit in Rome in November, 1996.

Mr. Gardner was previously a project manager at the Soviet Nonproliferation Project, a research and training program run by the Monterey Institute of International Studies in California. While there, he authored *Nuclear Nonproliferation: A Primer*. Mr. Gardner has also developed training materials for the World Bank. Mr. Gardner spent two years helping Peruvian womens' groups develop urban small livestock projects. He holds Master's degrees in Politics from Brandeis University, and in Public Administration from the Monterey Institute of International Studies. He received his Bachelor's degree from Santa Clara University.

Introduction

S ome 4,400 years ago, the city-states of ancient Sumer in modern-day Iraq faced an unsettling dilemma. Farmland was gradually accumulating salt, the byproduct of evaporating irrigation water. Almost imperceptibly, the salt began to poison the rich soil, and over time harvests tapered off.

Until 2400 BC, Sumerians had managed the problem of dwindling yields by cultivating new land, thereby ensuring the consistent food surpluses needed to support their armies and bureaucracies. But now they had reached the limits of agricultural expansion. And over the next three centuries, accumulating salts drove crop yields down more than 40 percent. The crippled production, combined with an ever-growing population, led to shrinking food reserves, which in turn reduced the ranks of soldiers and civil servants. By 1800 BC, Sumerian agriculture had effectively collapsed, and this once glorious civilization faded into obscurity.[1]

The decline of ancient Sumer holds valuable lessons for today's policymakers, who essentially follow the age-old practice of cultivating cropland until it is exhausted or taken for a new purpose. Around the world today, farmland continues to be devoured or damaged, with little appreciation of its finitude. Urban expansion, loss of irrigation water, and ongoing wear and tear to soils all claim valuable cropland each year. And since 1981 grainland, the base of world food production, has steadily disappeared. As opportunities to cultivate new lands dwindle, cropland losses loom increasingly large.

The casual official attitude toward cropland loss and

degradation is largely a consequence of farmers' mesmeriz-
ing success with intensive cultivation. Starting in the 1960s,
yields, especially of grain, rose so rapidly that they out-
weighed the simultaneous losses of arable land. Since 1984,
however, growth in grain yields has slowed—dramatically so
in the 1990s—and yield increases no longer fully compensate for the steady elimination of grainland. As in ancient
Sumer, sluggish productivity and loss of land are draining
food reserves: global grain stocks have fallen steadily since
1993, hitting a record low in 1996.

The double blow to food production—a shrinking supply of quality cropland, and lethargic growth in yields—
comes on the eve of the largest increase in food demand in
human history. In 25 years, farmers will be asked to feed 7.9
billion people, 39 percent more than they do today. Nine of
every ten new births will occur in developing countries,
where grain self-sufficiency fell from 96 percent in 1969–71
to 88 percent in 1993–95. In addition, economic expansion
in poor countries will allow millions to move from a monot-
onous diet heavy in starches to varied meals that include
livestock products, fruits and vegetables, and foods prepared
with vegetable oil. While these foods offer benefits to consumers and farmers, they also require more land to produce.
As people become wealthier, they have a disproportionate
effect on cropland because they draw on food stocks more
heavily than the poor do.[2]

The imminent jump in demand for food would seem to
dictate protection of agricultural resources—especially cropland—but it has not yet had that effect. Losses of cropland
continue to be serious, and they show no signs of abating.
Land-tight China, for example, lost nearly 4 million hectares
of cropland on a net basis—roughly 3 percent of the total
cropped area—between 1987 and 1992. Some of the land
was claimed by expanding cities, a source of attrition that is
projected to remain active: China hopes to build 600 *new*
cities by 2010, thus doubling the number it has now. Net
losses in the United States between 1982 and 1992 totaled
an area larger than the state of New Jersey, just under 2 mil-

lion hectares. Meanwhile, growth in irrigated cropland—the source of more than half of increased global production between the mid-1960s and the mid-1980s—has plateaued, and millions of hectares irrigated with non-renewable groundwater will almost certainly be lost from production. Finally, degradation of farmland continues largely unabated, threatening a repetition of the toll exacted since World War II. Between 1945 and 1990, erosion, salination, waterlogging, and other degradation eliminated from production an area equal to the cropland of two Canadas. In an increasingly land-tight world, and with demand for food rising dramatically, losses of this magnitude cannot be repeated without grave consequences.

Yield increases no longer fully compensate for the elimination of grainland.

As cropland is lost, a growing share of what remains is used for non-food crops such as cotton, tobacco, or corn for ethanol, or for luxury foods like coffee or cocoa, which increasingly compete for space with grain, the cornerstone of much of the world's diet. Meanwhile, the potential for agricultural expansion—which lies mostly in Africa and Latin America—is often overestimated, typically by including marginal land, where cultivation may not be sustainable. Indeed, the world's major grain producers have all damaged large areas of land in recent years through overexpansion, and many are now pulling back to a more sustainably cultivated area.

With little room for large-scale expansion, and with a big increase in food demand just around the corner, protection of sustainably farmable cropland is urgently required. While yields could conceivably regain their robust rates of growth of past decades, banking on this is risky. The yield trend this decade so far is not encouraging, and some of the ingredients that prompted the earlier surge in yields are now difficult to access—such as new irrigation water—or are dangerous to humans and ecosystems, such as pesticides. Continued tolerance of reckless losses of cropland will

increase the pressure on yields and the risk of supply failures.

Once policymakers begin to grasp the essential importance of cropland, a number of measures can be taken to
stem the losses and protect the quality of what remains.
Preservation programs in Europe and the United States have
saved millions of hectares of prime farmland from the bulldozer. Technologies for reducing erosion on all kinds of
fields are proven and could be more widely implemented.
And promising technologies to make agriculture more productive—and sustainable—can help reduce the pressures on
remaining agricultural land. But the challenge is pressing.
Future generations will urgently need the farmland that we
have long treated as an expendable commodity.

Trends: From Surplus to Scarcity

Human efforts to produce ever-greater amounts of food
reached a historic pinnacle in 1981. After thousands of
years of expansion, the amount of grainland under cultivation worldwide peaked, topping 732 million hectares.[a]
Between 1981 and 1995, in roughly a mirror image of its
steady climb, harvested grain area fell by 7.6 percent, before
rebounding in 1996; today it covers about as much area—
roughly 695 million hectares—as in 1974.[b] From the per-
spective of land use, the period after 1981 marks a new agricultural era, in which increasing demand for grain is met on
a generally contracting base of land.[5] (See Figure 1.)

---

a. Of the major crop categories—grain, fruits and vegetables, roots and
tubers, and oilseeds—grain is the most widely consumed, and is hence the
best barometer for agriculture. Direct and indirect (via livestock) consumption of grain account for well over half of human calorie intake.

b. "Harvested area" can be more or less than the physical area. A 100-
hectare (ha) farm that is harvested twice a year is registered as 200 ha of harvested area. Alternatively, 100 ha fallowed every other year is 50 ha of harvested area.

FIGURE 1

World Grain Harvested Area, 1950–96

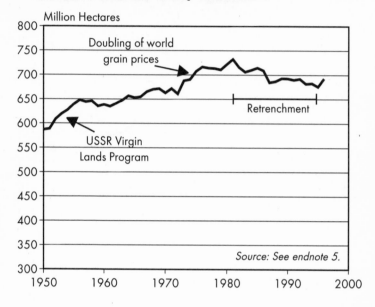

Source: See endnote 5.

This new era is the latest of three historical periods that highlight the changing role of land expansion in agriculture. In the first era, covering the 10,000 years that ended in the middle of this century, expansion of cultivated area was the chief tool for increasing food production. Cropland (which includes grainland) increased as population did, from the first plots farmed on the Anatolian Plateau in what is now Turkey to the 1.4 billion hectares under production globally in 1955. 'New land for new demand' sums up the food production strategy during the first era.

After World War II, global population increased rapidly, prompting the search for other ways to increase output, and spawning a second era. Cropland continued to expand, but this approach was now a minor source of growth in output, with the exception of two expansions—the Virgin Lands program in the USSR in the late 1950s, which brought some 30 million hectares of grainland into production, and the expansion prompted by the sharp run-up in grain prices

FIGURE 2

World Grain Harvested Area Per Person, 1950–96

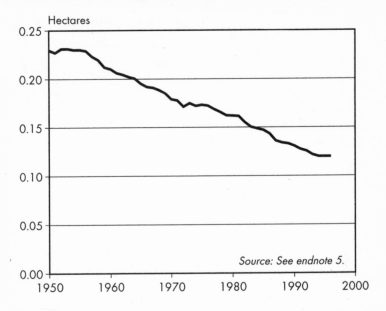

Source: See endnote 5.

in the mid-1970s. Yield increases became the principal tool for boosting production, accounting for nearly 80 percent of new output between 1950 and 1981. "Green Revolution" technologies—new crop varieties, pesticides, and increased use of fertilizer and irrigation—made each hectare more fruitful than pre-modern farmers would have imagined possible. Yield increases for grains even outpaced population growth, raising production per person during this period. In essence, rising yields became a strikingly effective substitute for land expansion.[6]

In the third (current) era, area expansion's contribution to new output has virtually ended. Except for a temporary increase in area in 1986, and an increase of unknown duration starting in 1996, area expansion has not been available to boost output. Indeed, as grain area has contracted, a startling change has become apparent: for the first time ever, the entire burden of increased grain production rests on yields alone. Not only is area expansion unavailable to assist in raising output, but net shrinkage in cropped area is a drag on production, which increases the pressure on yields still further.

Falling grain prices may account for some of the contraction in grain area in this third period. Prices of the major grains fell nearly continuously in the 1980s and early 1990s, giving farmers incentive to switch to crops such as fruits and vegetables, whose prices rose in the same period. Grain price increases in 1995-96 of more than 30 percent were sufficient to increase grain area by some 2.5 percent. If maintained, the higher prices might provoke more crop shifting, and coax out any remaining idle land. But should demand for fruits, vegetables, and other non-grain products remain strong, the potential for switching this area back to grains would be limited.[7]

By relying on a single source of growth—rising yields—today's global agricultural system is more vulnerable to supply failures than when area expansion was an option. Hints of this vulnerability appeared early in this third era, as yield increases began to falter. In 1985, and nearly every year since, grain yields have grown more slowly than global population, a reversal of the previous 35 years' experience, when average annual yield increases of more than 2 percent made food surpluses the norm. And as the 1990s unfolded, yield increases slackened further, handicapping agriculture's ability to keep up with current demand.[8]

The vulnerability of global agriculture is best illustrated by using the trend in cropland per person. Grain area per capita shrank by 30 percent between 1950 and 1981, to 0.16 hectares—less than a quarter the size of a soccer field. (See Figure 2.) Massive famine was avoided only because of robust yield growth, which compensated for the area loss. But by 1985, when yield growth began to falter, the combination of loss of area, slowing yield growth, and increasing population caused production per person to decline, ending a 34-year rising trend.[9]

Today, grain harvested area per person is 0.12 hectares—less than one-sixth of a soccer field—and falling.

Because yields no longer compensate for the continuing loss of land, a widening gap now separates the amount of food produced and the amount needed. This gap was closed between 1993 and 1995 by drawing down grain reserves, our global food savings account. Grain reserves averaged the equivalent of 81 days of global consumption between 1982 and 1993, but have fallen steadily since then, dropping to 48 days' worth in 1995. The gap was also minimized by a decline in grain consumption per person in several regions, especially the former Soviet Union (due to a severe depression), and Africa (due to deepening poverty). Clearly, however, neither reserves, nor depression, nor deepening poverty are sustainable or desirable solutions for ensuring an adequate food supply.[10]

The continuing decline in area per person will not end as long as global population continues to rise. But the contraction in area per person can be slowed by minimizing losses of land. Since the old reliance on area expansion is no longer possible, preserving existing, sustainably cropped farmland is a vital tool for helping farmers to answer the coming demand for food.

Expanding Cities

For millenia, cities have expanded into neighboring fields and orchards as their populations required more space for living, working, and playing. When land was plentiful, such expansion was easily accommodated, as farmers simply moved on to new plots. Today, cities are expanding rapidly, and because little new land is available for cultivation in the world's most crowded regions, cropland losses from urban expansion are typically net losses. Indeed, in many countries, the price for new industry, roads, houses, and recreational facilities can increasingly be measured in hectares of lost cropland.

Many competing claims to land are linked to the glob-

al rise of urbanization. Population growth and a preference
for city life combined with economic—often environmentally rooted—problems in rural areas have caused a massive
demographic shift to the world's urban areas. While fewer
than 30 percent of the world's people lived in cities in 1950,
more than 45 percent do today, and by 2025, the urban
share of global population is expected to surpass 60 percent.
The move to cities is not limited to the 100 or so megacities
that receive the greatest attention; the fastest urban expansion is found in the 30,000 or so medium-sized cities in
developing countries, where little or no planning guides the
growth process.[11]

Because many cities were founded in agricultural areas,
urban expansion often paves over farmland. The threat to
cropland can be substantial: more than half of all U.S. agricultural production, for example, comes from counties on
the edge of cities. Moreover, cropland near cities is often
highly fertile. In the United States just over 18 percent of all
rural land is classified as prime farmland; but within 50
miles of the largest urban areas, 27 percent is prime. And
because development of agricultural land is rarely reversed,
encroachment represents a permanent loss of a principal
agricultural resource.[12]

One of the engines driving urban expansion is economic growth, a primary national goal in every capital on
the planet. But in the world's most crowded regions, traditional economic growth has an increasingly evident down-
side: the serious loss of food production capacity. Growth
spurs those activities that can accelerate cropland loss,
including construction of factories, houses, and roads, and
development of recreational areas. Especially in Asia, where
economic growth has averaged more than 8 percent over the
past four years, this competition for land is increasingly evident.[13]

Urban and industrial growth on the Indonesian island
of Java, for example, is feverish. The U.S. Department of
Agriculture estimates that urban expansion claimed 20,000
hectares of cropland in 1994, an area large enough to supply

rice to 330,000 Indonesians. The losses are part of an ongoing boom. Population in the urban agglomeration that
encompasses Jakarta, the capital, ballooned by 44 percent in
the 1980s, from 11.9 million to 17.1 million. The accompa-
nying industrial growth boosted industry's hunger for land;
office space in Jakarta multiplied by 19 times between 1978
and 1992. Housing development has been still more land
intensive. Between 1983 and 1992, approved requests for
housing starts in just three cities in West Java—Bogor,
Tangerang, and Bekasi—covered nearly 61,000 hectares. It is
unclear what portion of this urban expansion came at agriculture's expense, but the share is likely to be quite high
since Java is one of the most densely populated areas in the
world, with little flat land to spare.[14]

The powerful lure of industrial development, despite
its toll on cropland, is vividly demonstrated by recent events
in Vietnam. Concern about cropland losses there, which
total a reported 20,000 hectares each year, prompted Prime
Minister Vo Van Kiet in March 1995 to ban conversions of
rice paddies to non-farm uses. Continued losses at the 1994
rate would strip Vietnam of more than 7 percent of its cropland in the next 25 years, even as its population increases by
some 40 percent. Yet despite his expressed commitment to
farmland preservation, the Prime Minister approved a
request in July 1995 to re-zone more than 6,300 hectares of
farmland around Hanoi for infrastructure and industrial
projects, most likely for construction of a Ford automobile
assembly plant.[15]

Perhaps the greatest losses, however, are experienced in
China, where economic growth has been measured in double digits each year since 1992. Data on losses of arable land
there, though incomplete, are startling. George Brown, a
political scientist at the University of Missouri, analyzed
official land use data and found that 6.5 million hectares of
arable land—some 5 percent of the national total—were
pulled from production in China in only six years, 1987
through 1992. (See Table 1.) Nearly two-thirds of these losses are unexplained, possibly because their conversion to

TABLE 1

Loss of Arable Land in China, 1987–92

Source of loss	Area lost	Share of China's Cropland
	(thousand hectares)	(percent)
Explained Losses	2317	1.8
National capital construction	508	0.4
Township & village collective construction	240	0.2
Peasant house building	184	0.1
Forest expansion	833	0.6
Pasture expansion	552	0.4
Unexplained losses	4239	3.3
Total	6556	5.0

Source: See Brown in endnote 16.

non-farm uses was illegal. Of the explained losses, 40 percent involved expansion of infrastucture, industry, and housing. Assuming that the unexplained losses can be accounted for in the same way, a total of 2.6 million hectares of land were surrendered to urbanization in the six-year period, an annual retreat of 433,000 hectares per year.[16]

For several reasons, China's reported loss of cropland most likely understates the extent of the problem. Chinese peasants historically have underreported the amount of land cultivated in order to reduce their tax assessment; therefore shrinkage of unreported land would not appear in official statistics. In addition, local officials began to be penalized in 1987 for losses of cropland in their jurisdiction, providing further incentive to underreport. Further, losses reported by the World Bank and independent researchers for the 1950s through the 1970s—before the pressures of rapid industrialization began—are actually higher than those reported by the Chinese government for the late 1980s and 1990s, suggesting government underreporting.[17]

China also brought new land into production during the 1987-92 period, but its net losses were still impressive, some 3.87 million hectares. This area represents a drop of 15 million tons of grain, enough to feed 45 million Chinese. The net losses are also impressive compared to the country's remaining potential for expansion. Experts estimate that China can hope to expand its cropped area by no more than 10 million hectares overall (and only at great expense). Continued losses at the 1987-92 rate would eliminate this expansion potential in just 15 years.[18]

While cropland loss to urban expansion is most critical in Asia, it is increasingly felt in other areas, even in land-rich countries. In the United States, where land is relatively abundant, two New York Cities' worth of cropland—some 168,000 hectares—were paved over each year between 1982 and 1992. The losses place at risk much of U.S. fruit and vegetable acreage. A study by the American Farmland Trust mapped urban growth against prime and unique farmland to identify areas with the highest likelihood of farmland loss. Rapid urbanization is underway in south Florida, California, and other areas that supply most of the nation's fruits and vegetables. In fact, the study found that more than 86 percent of U.S. fruit and 87 percent of vegetables are grown in rapidly urbanizing areas. Without protection of these areas, the United States could find itself exporting much less produce in coming decades. Such exports accounted for 35 percent of the U.S. agricultural trade surplus in 1995.[20]

California is a case in point. Its agricultural core, the Central Valley, is a highly productive, 300-mile-long cornucopia, supplying 8 percent of U.S. agricultural output (by value) on less than 1 percent of U.S. farmland. Indeed, six of the top ten agricultural counties in the United States are found in the valley; Fresno County alone, the most productive one in the nation, outproduces each of 24 U.S. *states*. But California is steadily losing agricultural land. Between 1984 and 1992, more than 125,000 hectares of its cropland—some 3 percent of the total cropped area—were con-verted to urban or other non-farm uses; more than a third of this land was prime farmland. The trend is a long-standing one in California: Los Angeles County, an urban agglomera-tion of more than 9 million people, was the most productive agricultural county in the United States at the end of World War II. The Santa Clara Valley, once acclaimed worldwide for its apricots, prunes, and other fruits, traded its orchards for industry, houses, and freeways, and has crowned its new image with a new name—Silicon Valley.[21]

In the U.S., two New York Cities' worth of cropland were paved over each year between 1982 and 1992.

Economic and population growth also stimulates expansion of transportation infrastructure, which can devour cropland. The interests of motorists and farmers are increasingly at odds as roads and parking lots pave over farmland. Automobile ownership is surging in Latin America, Eastern Europe, and especially Asia. In China, domestic car production has been growing at more than 15 percent annually; the government plans to increase automobile output from 1.4 million units in 1994 to 3 million in 2000. In Vietnam, import quotas for cars were tripled in 1996, and sales of four-wheel vehicles are projected to increase sixfold between 1995 and 2000. Vehicle sales and registrations are surging in India, Indonesia, Malaysia, and Thailand as well. Around Asia, the shift to transportation systems that emphasize private auto-mobiles is in full swing.[22]

Mass adoption of an automobile-centered transport system entails land costs that are often not appreciated. In the seven Asian nations for which road data are available, road area would need to expand by more than 4 million hectares to handle the increase in cars newly registered between 1989 and 1994 without increasing congestion. If these additional roads were built, and if three-quarters of the area were taken from cropland, area sufficient to satisfy the grain needs of some 30 million people would be lost. The likelihood that a large share of the new road space would come from cropland is high, given the lack of spare land in Asia, and because roads and agriculture are most economical and function best on the same kind of terrain, typically, flat valley bottoms.[23]

Urbanization and rising prosperity also spark demand for recreational space. Golf, an increasingly popular but land-intensive pastime, is spreading rapidly in Asia. In Thailand, 160 golf courses were built between 1989 and 1994, averaging one every eleven days. If construction followed the same pattern it did prior to 1988, two-thirds of these were built on agricultural land. At 160 to 320 acres each, the golf courses most likely displaced between 17,000 and 34,000 hectares—an area that, if planted in grain, would have supported hundreds of thousands of people. In other Asian countries, golf's effect on agriculture is less well known, but the large number of new courses in densely populated countries is bound to take a toll on farmland. South Korea's 86 operating golf courses in 1993-94 were to be augmented by 200 under construction and another 200 awaiting approval. And in the early 1990s, land-poor Japan, with 2,016 courses covering an area larger than metropolitan Tokyo, had 395 courses under construction or with permits to begin construction.[24]

Urbanization, the umbrella concept covering most of these causes of land loss, is projected to continue at a brisk pace into the next century. By the year 2000, for the first time in human history, more than half of us will live in cities, making continued pressure on cropland likely. If land per urban resident in developing countries is estimated at 0.05 hectares, some 50 million hectares will be needed there for urban expansion by 2010. Not all of this area will be developed at the expense of cropland, but in crowded regions such as South Asia and East Asia, net farmland losses are likely to be quite high. In South Asia, for example, where the potential for cropland expansion is widely believed to be virtually nil, urban population is projected to increase by some 420 million people between 1995 and 2010, implying an increase in urban area of some 21 million hectares. Urban expansion of this magnitude, in already crowded conditions, would inevitably lead to large losses of cropland.[25]

The continuing urbanization of China, home to more than one-fifth of the human family, is expected to be especially striking. China's Vice Minister of Construction has asserted that China hopes to build nearly 600 new cities by 2010, swelling the number from 633 in 1996 to 1,200 over the next 15 years. If this construction prompts cropland losses to industry, infrastructure and housing at the rate experienced between 1987 and 1993, about 6.5 million hectares—another 5 percent of China's agricultural land— would be lost from production by 2010, even as population there rises by some 14 percent.[26] Projections of cropland loss from urban growth in California are striking as well. At the 1984-92 rate of loss, California over the next 25 years would add more than 393,000 hectares—nearly 10 percent of its cropland—to the 125,000 already lost to urban and other uses.[27]

The pressure on cropland from the frenzy of urban and industrial activity makes some loss nearly inevitable. But the actual amount of this loss will depend on the development choices made by local and national governments, especially in crowded regions. Decisions about transportation, housing, industrial development, and recreation all affect land use, and they can be made more "cropland friendly."

Evaporating Irrigated Land

Of all cropland losses, the disappearance of irrigated land is perhaps most troubling, because this land has accounted for the lion's share of yield increases in recent decades. Yet losses of irrigated area now appear to offset meager gains—irrigation expansion, which slowed over the past two decades, has finally petered out entirely. Continued losses are likely, as agricultural water supplies are depleted, polluted, or claimed by other sectors.

Because irrigation makes it possible for water to be applied when crops need it and in the amounts they need, it allows two or even three crops to be planted in one year. The result is impressive productivity: irrigated land, while only 16 percent of cropland worldwide, provides some 40 percent of the world's food. This abundant output, combined with steady expansion of irrigated area in the 1960s and brisk expansion in the 1970s, made irrigation the source of more than half of the increase in global food production between the mid-1960s and the mid-1980s.[28]

Given the clear importance of irrigated land, losses of this resource are especially troubling. According to Food and Agriculture Organization (FAO) data, global irrigated area turned a corner in 1993 (the last year for which data are available), declining slightly after a nearly unbroken series of annual increases that had lasted several decades. This contraction culminates a long-standing deceleration of growth in irrigated area, from its peak rate of 2.3 percent per year between 1972 and 1975, to about 1 percent per year between 1982 and 1992. If yield increases are the primary engine driving growth in global food production, irrigation expansion—the oil that lubricates that engine—is now in short supply.[29]

Loss of irrigated cropland happens for many reasons. The end of irrigation subsidies in some republics of the former Soviet Union (FSU) following the dissolution of the USSR, for example, led to a massive shrinkage of irrigated area. Russia alone lost more than 700,000 hectares of irrigated cropland—some 13 percent of its irrigated area—between 1990 and 1993. The contraction in the FSU is expected to continue, possibly for another decade, until governments in the region recover their fiscal health.[30]

In California, urbanization is increasingly to blame for irrigation losses. Whereas 18 percent of the state's new urban land was developed on irrigated area in 1988-90, the share jumped to 24 percent in 1992-94. In all, irrigated area fell by some 25,000 hectares in California between 1990 and 1992, a loss of nearly 1 percent. This innocent-sounding rate, if continued, would eliminate almost 9 percent of irrigated land in California over the next 25 years.[31]

Reversing the downward trend in irrigated area per person will be difficult given the ongoing threats to land that is currently irrigated. In several regions with irrigated farming, depleted groundwater, polluted water supplies, and competition from non-farm sectors are reducing the agricultural water supply. All represent an emerging threat to cropland.

Groundwater depletion is an especially serious problem for irrigated agriculture. When groundwater is pumped faster than it is replenished, aquifers are depleted or become expensive to pump as water tables drop. Cropland that depends on such overpumped water is unsustainably farmed. The global extent of the problem has not been documented, but clues from the literature allow us to piece together estimates of crop area affected for some regions. At least 5 percent, and as much as 8 percent of global irrigated area depends to some degree on overpumped water; this conservative estimate is based on data from the Arabian Peninsula, Libya, northern China, northern India, Iran, and the High Plains and California in the United States; it does not include Pakistan or other areas whose agriculture depends on overdrafting. If the overpumping continues, and the supply of irrigated water is reduced, areas with a small fraction of overpumped water will suffer decreased yields, while areas that rely heavily on overdrafted water could be lost from production entirely.[32]

Where aquifers are too deep to be replenished by rainfall, as on much of the Arabian Peninsula and in Libya, the

> **At least 5 percent of global irrigated area depends to some degree on overpumped water.**

share of unsustainably pumped water applied to cropland is very high. Some 75 percent of the water used in agriculture on the Arabian Peninsula, for example, is not replenished. And because much of the land under cultivation cannot be sustained without irrigation, agriculture in these regions will face severe cutbacks in irrigated area when these "fossil" aquifers are depleted, assuming that other sources of irrigation water are not found. In the case of the Arabian Peninsula, this shrinkage could amount to 4 million hectares, and in Libya, more than 2 million hectares.[33]

Where aquifers are renewable, lowered yields and loss of area can be avoided if farmers adopt conservation practices or water-efficient technologies, or if they switch to less water-intensive crops. These measures have their limits, however. On the Texas High Plains between 1974 and 1989, irrigated area fell by more than 25 percent despite a decrease in water use per hectare of some 17 percent. Overdrafting was not responsible for the entire loss—high energy prices and falling food prices also made pumping uneconomical— but the decline in the water table was a contributing factor.[34]

In other places, competition for water, rather than a diminishing supply, is the principal threat to agricultural water. Cities increasingly vie with farmers for water, and in arid areas urban claims can lead directly to cropland loss. In Mexico City, for instance, urban growth has prompted the city to import nearly a third of its water from outside the Basin of Mexico (in which the city is located). This policy has lowered water tables in the nearby Lerma and Cutzamala basins, and is rapidly eliminating traditional agriculture from the nearby town of Xochimilco. In Jakarta, city dwellers extract groundwater at roughly three times the rate of recharge, which has restricted water supply to rice farmers north of the city, limiting rice production. In China, where some 200 cities are water deficient, water law gives urban and industrial users priority over farmers, with predictable effects for the agricultural sector. In the spring of 1996, when an oil field at Dongying on the Yellow River was in desperate need of water to continue operations, armed guards were posted along a 400-mile stretch of the Yellow River to prevent farmers from using river water for irrigation.[35]

Even where new water supplies are developed for farmers, their access to it is not guaranteed. In Thailand, a series of dams and irrigation infrastructure known as the Greater Chao Phrya Project helped farmers to increase the share of their land that was cultivated more than once per year, from 40 percent of cropped area in 1975 to 70 percent by the late 1980s. But farmers' increased use of water reduced the flow of the Chao Phrya River—the source of water for many cities, including Bangkok—by some 25 percent in the same period. As urban growth and industrial activity increased, so did urban thirst, prompting competition and conflict with farmers, who had less political clout than their city cousins. In 1989, some 160,000 hectares of crops planted in the dry season were lost when insufficient reservoir water was released to farmers. And in 1993 the government banned the planting of second crops in an effort to conserve water. Restrictions on agriculture due to water shortages are undoubtedly responsible for some of the 15 percent decline in Thai harvested grain area between 1985 and 1995.[36]

In the western United States, some cities and towns now purchase or lease irrigation water in order to assure sufficient urban supplies. Tucson, Arizona, for example, bought more than 9,300 hectares of farmland in the 1970s and 1980s in order to secure rights to water. Colorado Springs has purchased the rights to 18.2 million cubic meters of water, about a third of which is currently leased back to farmers, awaiting the time when Colorado Springs will need it. In California, Oregon, Washington, and Idaho, water is more commonly leased by cities than purchased. Under this arrangement, cities buy temporary rights to water, typically exercising their leasing option in years of low rainfall. Such leasing by the Palo Verde Irrigation District and the Metropolitan Water District of Southern California idled some 20,000 acres of farmland between 1992 and 1994.[37]

In some regions, agricultural water is polluted before it is depleted or claimed by others, resulting in loss of agricultural productivity and, in extreme cases, loss of cropland. In coastal regions, aquifers are often vulnerable to invasion by seawater as water tables drop, rendering the fresh water unfit for agricultural production. In Israel, for example, average salt levels in the coastal aquifer have increased by some 50 percent over the past 25 years; already, 10 percent of wells there yield water that is too salty for use on crops. In southern Suarashtra in India, thousands of hectares of land have been damaged by use of salty water from a polluted coastal aquifer, and in Haryana, 65 percent of the state sits over salty groundwater. In China, widespread water pollution from industrial sources is affecting the agricultural water supply as well. The Ministry of Agriculture reports that use of untreated waste water on crops accounts for the loss of over 5 million tons of grain annually, more than 1 percent of the harvest.[38]

The decline in irrigated area and the threat to agricultural water supplies raises the question of potential for irrigation expansion. Limits to enlargement are many and serious. In more and more regions, from the Middle East to parts of Asia to the American Southwest, water for expansion is simply unavailable. By 2020, assuming continued current rates of use per person, the ranks of nations that use more than 100 percent of their annual renewable water supply (by overpumping groundwater) will expand from ten to fifteen, most of them in the Middle East and North Africa. To supply a modest grain ration just to the quarter billion people born in the Middle East and North Africa over the next 25 years will nearly require another Nile River, some 76 billion cubic meters per year. Meanwhile, in North China, water deficits are expected to reach 35 billion cubic meters by 2020 unless new sources are developed. Because agriculture uses more than 80 percent of the region's water, adjustments to water shortages will rest heavily on the shoulders of farmers.[39]

Where water is accessible, the economic incentive to

develop new resources may be missing. One reason for the slow expansion of irrigation since the mid-1970s was the combination of falling food prices and rising irrigation construction costs, which made investments in irrigation uneconomical. If the world is entering a food-scarce era with rising food prices, investment in irrigation may again become attractive in some areas with sufficient water.[40]

In an increasingly crowded world, however, construction of the large dams usually required to make irrigation possible often entails a high social cost, as people are relocated to make room for a reservoir and its supporting infrastructure. Increasingly, the numbers of people involved are sizable: for the Three Gorges Dam under construction in China, more than a million people are being relocated. Where displaced people are poor, they have few options to resist the move, or to ensure that conditions in their new villages are no worse than the conditions they left.[41]

Given all these obstacles, irrigated area is expected to expand very slowly in coming decades. One study projects growth of only 0.3 percent annually over the next 50 years, roughly a third the rate of the decelerating 1980s, and only one eighth the peak growth rate of the mid-1970s. It is quite possible that no significant expansion will occur at all. Such poor prospects make halting the loss of irrigated land especially urgent.[42]

Degrading Our Future

Nearly everywhere, the greatest threat to cropland comes not from a bulldozer or city water manager, but from a less visible and more diffuse source: land degradation. Around the world, agriculture has eroded, compacted, contaminated, salted, or waterlogged extensive tracts of cropland, and the damage continues almost unabated today. Because most of this degradation is unseen, the threat it poses to agriculture is commonly underestimated. Yet the collapse of civilizations from the Sumerian 3,800 years ago to the Mayan in the ninth century—attributed in part to the loss of quality agricultural land—is testimony to the fundamental importance of soil health.

Data on the global extent of degradation and its toll on productivity, though sketchy, is worrisome. A 1990 United Nations study on land degradation estimated that 552 million hectares—equal to a full 38 percent of today's global cultivated area—had been damaged to some degree by agricultural mismanagement since World War II. (See Table 2.) The study is the first global-scale demonstration that soil—the very foundation of agriculture—is under siege around the world. Actually, the report may understate the extent of the damage. A 1994 study of South Asia that compared the UN findings with more localized studies of agricultural degradation in the region estimated that soil damage extends to some 10 percent more area than the UN study had indicated.[43]

In the worst cases, degradation has actually taken land out of production. In the UN study, soils described as "strongly" or "extremely" degraded—either beyond restoration or requiring major engineering work to restore their productivity—accounted for more than 15 percent of the world's damaged cropland. This lost area, some 86 million hectares, roughly equals Canada's cropped area twice over. If it were producing grain at average yields for the 1990s, it could feed some 775 million people, about 13 percent of today's global population. Despite the gravity of such losses, degradation severe enough to pull land from production continues today, and may be on the increase: while annual losses between 1945 and 1990 averaged just under 2 million hectares, various sources suggest that today's losses range from 5 to 10 million hectares per year.[44]

Most degraded land, however, is still in production, though much of it is less fertile than it used to be. Productivity losses to degradation have not been measured on a global scale, but some rough calculations have been made. Using productivity losses for each degradation category

TABLE 2

Share of Agricultural Land with Degraded Soils, 1945–90

Region	Australia	Europe	North America	Asia	South America	Africa	Central America
Degraded share (percent)	16	25	26	38	45	65	74

Source: See Oldeman in endnote 44.

established in the UN study, the approximate drop in output from degraded soils can be calculated. This exercise indicates that lightly and moderately degraded lands yielded on the order of 10 percent less in 1990 than they would have without degradation. When strongly and extremely degraded (non-productive) lands are added to these reversals, the production loss from all degradation rises to more than 18 percent. In a world of increasingly tight land supplies and steadily increasing food demand, these retreats assume growing significance.[45]

The thin layer of earth we call topsoil is essential to land's fertility. Typically only some 15 centimeters deep, topsoil is a rich medium containing organic matter, minerals, nutrients, insects, microbes, worms and other elements needed to provide a nurturing environment for plants. While fertilizer offers a short-term fix to soil productivity, it replaces only the soil's nutrients, not the entire spectrum of elements that make up the soil community, all of which are needed for long-term health.

Erosion, the most pervasive form of soil degradation (accounting for 84 percent of degraded areas in the UN study), robs the world of a natural patrimony that is formed at only a glacial pace. The typical hectare accumulates only 1 ton or so (a few millimeters) of new soil each year. Net erosion (the amount worn away from a hectare, less the amount that is washed or blown to it from a different hectare) is difficult to measure, but the highest rates of gross

TABLE 3

Selected Examples of Soil Degradation

Country	Extent of Degradation
China	Erosion affects more than a third of China's territory—some 3.67 million square kilometers. In Guangxi province, more than a fifth of irrigation systems are destroyed or completely silted up by eroded soils. Salination has lowered crop yields on 7 million hectares, use of untreated urban sewage has seriously damaged some 2.5 million hectares, and nearly 7 million hectares are polluted by industrial wastes.
Russia	Eroded area increases by 400,000-500,000 hectares each year, and now affects two-thirds of Russia's arable land. Water erosion has created some 400,000 gullies covering more than 500,000 hectares.
Iran	Nearly all—94 percent—of Iran's agricultural land is estimated to be degraded, the bulk of it to a moderate or strong degree. Salination affects some 16 million hectares of farmland, and has forced at least 8 million hectares from production.
Pakistan	Gullies occupy some 60 percent of the 1.8 million hectare Pothwar Plateau. More than 16 percent of agricultural land suffers from salination. In all, more than 61 percent of agricultural land is degraded.
India	Degradation affects one-quarter of India's agricultural land. Erosion associated with shifting cultivation has denuded approximately 27,000 square kilometers of land east of Bihar. At least 2 million hectares of salinized land have been abandoned.

Haiti	32 percent of land is suitable for farming, but 61 percent is farmed. Severe erosion eliminated 6,000 hectares of cropland per year in the mid-1980s.
Australia	More than 4.5 million hectares of drylands—10 percent of all cropland—and more than 8 percent of irrigated area are affected by salting. Area affected by dryland salting doubled in size between 1975 and 1989.

Source: See endnote 47.

erosion are certainly many times greater than the rate of creation. Reports of losses exceeding 100 tons per hectare are common for individual plots, especially on sloping terrain, in many developing nations.[46]

In the developing world, erosion and poverty interact in a destructive cycle: erosion is often rooted in poverty and crowding, while poverty and crowding are often the harvest of erosion. The UN's 1990 degradation study asserts that overgrazing, deforestation, agricultural mismanagement, and overharvesting of fuelwood—activities carried out disproportionately by poor people—account for 70 percent of damage done to the world's soil. These problems, in turn, are often related to a skewed distribution of land. Inadequate access to land pushes poor farmers onto small plots of marginal quality which they cultivate more intensively than the soil can bear, or without the investments needed to use it sustainably.[48]

Because the best valley land in much of the world was claimed long ago for agriculture or other purposes, more and more poor farmers are retreating to hillsides, an ecologically vulnerable topography because of its great potential for erosion. Around the world, 160 million hectares of hillside land—more than 11 percent of the world's cropland—were identified in 1989 as "severely eroded" in areas as diverse as the highlands of Ethiopia, the uplands of the Andes and

Himalayas, and the central highlands of Central America. With rising population densities, the threat to mountain plots has grown. In the Philippines, cultivated upland forest area increased from less than 10 percent of total cultivated area in 1960 to more than 30 percent in 1987, according to a World Resources Institute report. And while cropped area in the Philippine lowlands expanded only by 1.9 percent between 1980 and 1987, hillside cropped area expanded by 7.6 percent.[49]

Another type of marginal agricultural land subject to increasing stress is farmland cut from tropical forests. Tropical soils are low in fertility, and can be cultivated successfully only with long fallow periods, typically 20-25 years. As land pressures increase, farmers are forced to cultivate fallowed land before it has completed its full rest period. In tropical regions of Africa and Southeast Asia, where fallow periods were once measured in decades, land is now idled for just a few years, not enough to fully recover fertility.[50]

The extent of pressure on marginal lands is difficult to quantify, but some approximations have been made. A 1989 study estimated that 370 million very poor people live in "low potential" rural areas, regions of low soil productivity that are probably environmentally sensitive. Another study asserts that 300 million people worldwide practice shifting cultivation, which depends on adequate fallowing. To the extent that areas with "low potential" and those subject to shifting cultivation are experiencing population pressures on the land, the result is likely to be increased degradation.[51]

Another form of soil degradation, salination, affects a much less extensive area than erosion does. But because this damage is common on irrigated land—which is especially productive—salination carries disproportionate importance. A 1995 study, drawing on national and global data from the 1980s, estimated that 20 percent of the world's irrigated area suffers from salination. Because the investments needed to flush salts from irrigated land are often not undertaken, salination severe enough to remove land from production is still common, claiming an estimated 1.5-2.5 million hectares annually.   And salinized land that remains in production often yields poorly, just as it did in ancient Sumer. In the Central Asian republics, for example, salination is blamed for declining cotton yields: fields that produced 2.8 tons per hectare of cotton in the late 1970s were yielding only 2.3 tons in the late 1980s, despite increased use of fertilizer.[52]

Notwithstanding the adoption of conservation measures in some parts of the world, damage to land, especially from erosion, is still a serious problem on all continents. If the most severe degradation—which leads to cropland abandonment—continues at its 1945-90 rate, some 47 million hectares will be lost by 2020. Meanwhile, productivity on most of the remaining damaged lands will likely continue to decline.   Such losses, which were manageable in a less crowded world, can no longer be tolerated.[53]

Changing Tastes

E ven as cities, industry, and poor farm management consume agricultural land, changes *within* agriculture are affecting cropland use. Increased incomes in poor countries are shifting food demand and altering the mix of crops under production, while a growing number of industrial uses for crops raise industry's claim to agricultural products. In terms of nurturing human beings, the new patterns arguably represent a less efficient use of land than previous patterns did, thus increasing the pressure on a limited agricultural land base.

Grain production dominates land use, because grain yields a higher level of protein and calories per hectare, in a combination that meets human needs, than any other major food group. Yet as non-grains and non-food crops have claimed expanded areas, grainland's share of total cropland has fallen in recent years, from just over half of global cropped area in 1980 to just over 47 percent in 1994. Thus, even as the global cropped area shrinks, the most efficient crop group—grains—is claiming a smaller portion.[54]

During most of the 1980-94 period, the shift away from grains was undoubtedly assisted by the decline in grain prices as well as increases in the prices of other crops, such as fruits and vegetables. To this extent, land devoted to alternative crops might be viewed as "reserve grainland," which can be switched back to grain if this commodity becomes scarce. But if developing country economies continue to strengthen, the demand for alternative crops is likely to remain strong. Meeting the growing demand for both grain and non-grain crops will be a growing challenge, the more so if quality cropland continues to be lost.

As grainland area declined by 9 percent after 1981, a variety of non-grain crops surged. Although they still claim less land than grains do, the expansion in the area they occupy is cause for concern. The largest gains in area were seen in oilseeds, especially soybeans, whose global coverage increased by some 22 percent between 1981 and 1994. Soybeans are used primarily to produce cooking oil and livestock feed, the demand for which increases with rising incomes. In the 1960s and 1970s, prosperity in industrialized countries fueled growth in soybean output, especially for feed production. Production plateaued in the late 1970s and early 1980s, but another surge began in the mid-1980s, this one largely fueled by rising incomes in developing countries. In these places, fried foods (e.g., fried rice) and meat, once luxuries beyond the reach of the poorest, appeared more frequently as incomes climbed, a welcome change in diet facilitated by increased soybean production.[55] (See Figure 3.)

Like grain, soybeans deliver high levels of calories and protein per hectare, but soybeans are more land hungry than grain, for two reasons. First, soybean yields have grown more slowly than grain yields over the past three decades, so a hike in demand for soybeans is more likely to

FIGURE 3

World Soybean Harvested Area, 1950–95

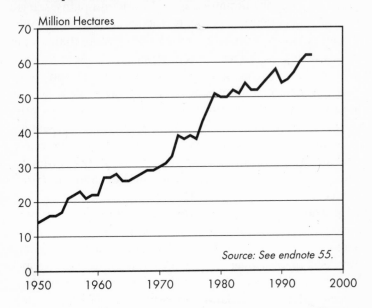

Source: See endnote 55.

require an increase in area than is the case for grain. Indeed, while yield growth accounted for the entire rise in grain production since 1981, less than half of the increase in soybean output in the period was yield driven; the rest came from expanded area. Without a substantial jump in yields, continued growth in soybean demand will create a need for increasingly larger area for soybean production. And in a land-tight world, the expanded soybean area may come at the expense of our staple crops, grains.[56]

Soybeans also intensify the pressure on agricultural land for a more indirect reason. Roughly 70 percent of soybean production is used for meal, most of which is fed to livestock. By comparison, less than 40 percent of grain production goes to livestock. Thus, while soybeans yield high levels of calories and protein per hectare, only a fraction of their food value is passed along to humans.[57]

Another set of crops whose production surged as grainland area contracted over the past 15 years is fruits and vegetables. Data is sketchy for these products, but between 1980 and 1994 global area gains of more than 15 percent were registered for tomatoes, cauliflower, pumpkins, squash, green peppers, onions, garlic, carrots, and melons, with five of these crops posting area expansions of more than 25 percent. Again, the increases were especially evident in countries with rapidly rising incomes: China, for example, home to the hottest economy, saw fruit and vegetable area more than double between 1980 and 1993. These crops bring variety and vitamins to a diet, but relatively few calories and little protein, which are of basic nutritional importance. They are a significant complement to grains, but if they displace grainland, the output of calories and protein is reduced.[58]

The diversification of food demand brought on by rising incomes is seen in a range of other products as well. Non-essential foods and non-food crops all required large increases in area over the past 15 years. By 1994, coffee, chocolate, sugarcane, tea, tobacco, and cotton claimed 4.1 percent of total cropland, up from 3.4 percent in 1980. Crops for industrial use also took more area. Natural, biodegradable crop materials were seen as environmentally superior substitutes for petroleum-based products. Bio-based resins, for example, are substitutes for plastic packaging, citrus oils are used in adhesives and solvents, and dairy products now have pharmaceutical applications. Ethanol, a fuel made from corn, required roughly 9 percent of the area planted to corn in the United States in 1995, a 52 percent increase over the amount of land used for this purpose in 1990.[59]

The newly prosperous cannot be blamed for desiring a more varied diet, nor should environmentally superior industrial products be discouraged. If incomes continue to rise in the developing world, and if the demand for more environmentally friendly materials increases, the area needed to meet a more diverse demand for food is also likely to continue to rise, even before population increases are factored in. In a land-scarce world, the area sown with our staple crops—grains—could continue to be affected. By reducing losses in cropland, the world's capacity to meet this increasingly diverse demand will be strengthened.

A Land-Scarce World

Without a large increase in cropped area or a dramatic surge in yields, ongoing population pressures and continuing losses of cropland will literally squeeze the agricultural land base dry. Yet the potential for expansion is small, especially compared with the coming need for increased production.

Given projected increases in population in coming decades, the amount of cropland per person will certainly continue to fall. Today's grain area per person of 0.12 hectares will drop to 0.10 hectares by 2010, and to 0.09 hectares by 2020, assuming that grain area stabilizes at 700 million hectares. (See Figure 4.) Every person added to the human family, and every hectare of land lost, places additional pressure on scientists and farmers to grow more on less land. Whether scientists and farmers can once again compensate for the shrinking area per person as they did before 1985 remains to be seen. Meanwhile, as grain area per person ratchets downward, the need to protect the cropland base becomes more pressing.[60]

The continuing loss of agricultural land raises the question of potential for renewed expansion of agricultural area. Nowhere is the potential great, especially relative to the coming food demand. Even in those regions with large expanses of untouched wilderness, several obstacles to expansion remain, above all, the need to protect vital environmental services such as water storage and erosion control. In many cases, conversion of ecosystems to cropland would eliminate ecosystem services that are worth more than the food that could be generated from the same land.

National experience with agricultural expansion

demonstrates that land cannot be sustainably farmed just anywhere. The world's major grain-producing regions now recognize the environmental error of overextending cropland, and have initiated programs to return marginal farmland to more environmentally sustainable uses, such as grazing. In the former Soviet Union, for example, land originally brought into cultivation in the 1954-62 Virgin Lands Campaign is now being returned to pasture, its previous use. The contraction is especially dramatic in Kazakhstan, where harvested grain area has fallen 24 percent since the mid-1980s, from 25 million hectares to only 18.4 million. With eroded soils and scant rainfall, the abandoned land had yielded only one-fifth the world average for grains. Grainland area is forecast to stabilize at some 13-16 million hectares, just one-half to two-thirds of the mid-1980s peak area.[61]

In the United States, much of the grain area added in the 1970s—when grain prices doubled and the government exhorted farmers to plant "fencerow to fencerow"—has been returned to its natural state. Under the Conservation Reserve Program, some 15 million hectares of marginal land—approximately equal to the expansion area in the mid-1970s—were removed from production under ten-year contracts. And 40,000 hectares now devoted to sugar cane in Florida's Everglades will be returned to natural wetlands under a plan approved in 1996 by the Congress in an attempt to reverse the pollution of regional water supplies, which are contaminated by fertilizer and pesticide runoff.[62]

Cropland lost to urban expansion in China grabs the headlines, but much of the country's vanishing farmland has been turned back to forest and pasture in recent years. Between 1987 and 1992, some 45 percent of converted cropland was reforested or converted to grazing land. Farmers and officials recognized that these lands were of minimal value as cropland, but could be used more profitably for wood harvesting and meat production. In their natural state they could also protect against erosion, retain water in their soils, and provide other important environmental services.[63]

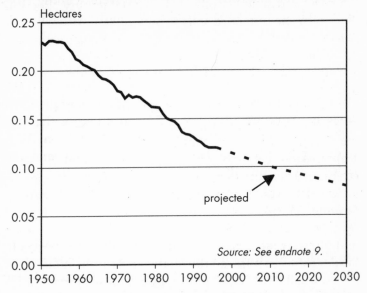

FIGURE 4

World Grain Harvested Area Per Person, 1950–2030

Hectares

projected

Source: See endnote 9.

For these three nations, and for India and Europe as well—which together supply two-thirds of the world's grain—little potential for expansion exists. If Europe could release for production the 10 percent of its cropland set aside in 1996, and if the United States were to re-open (and carefully farm) 7 million hectares of the least sensitive land set aside under the Conservation Reserve Program, some 11 million hectares would be added to the global stock of land, enough to feed 150 million people—just 20 months' worth of world population growth.[64]

In Africa and Latin America, the potential for expansion appears to be greater, but is not likely to be extensive. Much of the area in these regions lacks the prerequisites for successful farming: a dependable supply of water, roads and processing facilities, and institutional underpinnings such as credit and secure land titling. Above all, poor-quality soils will inhibit expansion. According to the FAO, more than 70 percent of land with agricultural potential in Sub-

Saharan Africa and Latin America is handicapped by unfa-
vorable agricultural conditions such as steep slopes, poor
drainage, and shallow soils. Low natural fertility affects 42
percent of the untapped soils in Sub-Saharan Africa, and 46
percent in Latin America. Even if the infrastructure and
institutional support for farming remote regions were made
available, the viability of such an effort would remain in
doubt.[65]

Brazil's attempt to colonize the Amazon region in the
1970s is a clear demonstration of the difficulty of introduc-
ing farming to remote regions with poor soils. The
Transamazon colonization scheme, announced in 1970,
envisioned construction of a highway through the Amazon
jungle that would open millions of hectares of forest for
farming. The plan foresaw resettlement of a million families
by 1980. But by 1978, only 7,600 families had been settled
and turnover rates were high, as the scheme was plagued by
lack of infrastructure, administrative difficulties, and, above
all, poor soil fertility. Tropical soils like those in the Amazon
are notoriously meager in nutrients, and can be farmed sustainably only with long fallow periods. In the late 1970s,
rice yields in the resettled areas were less than half of the
U.S. average, and well below the world average. Much of the
land that could not sustain ongoing, intensive cultivation,
was converted to grazing land or abandoned; by 1980 the
program was sharply curtailed.[66]

Similarly, current attempts to claim land for farming
on some of Indonesia's islands are encountering more difficulty than anticipated. By the year 2000, the government
plans to resettle over 10 million families on more than 20
million hectares, thereby expanding Indonesian cropped
area by roughly two-thirds. The ambitious plan may be still-
born, however, if the experience of the first settlers is any
indication. Because of a shortage of water in the dry season,
settlers on the island of Sumatra and Kalimantan are largely
unable to double-crop their rice as planned. Other settlers
have received land plagued by poor drainage and low organic content; despite heavy applications of fertilizer and other

inputs, yields are very low.[67]

Moreover, most of the new Indonesian farmland is cut from forests. In addition to conserving water and soil, forests perform other valuable environmental services. They play host to a rich diversity of species that may hold the key to future advances in agriculture and medicine, for instance.

Forests also store vast amounts of carbon, typically absorbing 20-50 times more than crops and pastures do; clearing them for agriculture triggers a huge net release of carbon, a greenhouse gas, into the atmosphere. For these reasons, and because tropical soils are poor in nutrients, clearing tropical forests for agriculture typically entails high environmental costs and relatively little gain. What appears to be a large expansion of Indonesian agriculture may—if completed—be better described as large-scale environmental devastation.[68]

The world's major grain-producing regions recognize the error of overextending cropland.

In this context, some calculations of potential expansion are unrealistically optimistic. The FAO, for example, estimates that 93 million hectares (124 million hectares of harvested area) are available for agricultural expansion in developing nations (except China) between 1990 and 2010, most of it in Sub-Saharan Africa and Latin America. However, the estimate is strictly a technical one that leaves aside the question of infrastructural and institutional capacity. It may also include forested area (their data cannot determine this), and much of the uncultivated area is of poor quality. The estimate depends, too, on an optimistic projection of irrigation expansion, at a time when irrigated area may have peaked. One clue that the FAO projection is overly sanguine is the recent track record of grain area: with a quarter of the FAO projection period passed, grain harvested area actually declined.[69]

One possible source of land that may already be counted in the FAO reserve is underutilized land on large haciendas. Data from some Latin American nations suggest that the intensity of land use becomes smaller and smaller as land holdings get larger and larger. In Brazil in 1980, for example, the share of land fallowed by the largest landholders was 11 times greater than the share fallowed by the small ones. These data are insufficient to determine the degree of underutilization on large farms—this would require knowledge of specific land characteristics, and the smallest farms may be cultivated *too* intensively in any case. But the large differences in intensity of use suggest that the scope for more intensive cultivation is indeed great.[70]

Whatever the potential for future expansion, the world will need all the land it can sustainably farm—along with steady yield increases—to meet the coming global food demand. Population growth alone will require a 50 percent increase in food production by 2030. If incomes in developing countries continue to climb, the need for extra food will grow still further because rising incomes among poor people usually spur an increase in demand for livestock products and oilseeds, two land-intensive sets of food. The more meat, milk, and cheese people eat, the greater the demand for grain, because these products are grain intensive. For example, 2 kilos of grain are required to produce a kilo of chicken or fish, 4 kilos go into a kilo of pork, and 7 kilos are needed for a kilo of feedlot-raised beef. Likewise, affluence boosts the demand for oilseeds, such as soybeans, a crop that relies on area expansion to a greater extent than grain does to meet increased demand. Rising incomes also boost the demand for vegetables and for beverage crops. Together with population increases, rising incomes portend a food system that is increasingly land hungry.[71]

Future cropland needs will depend on the level of food demand and on future yield trends—neither of which can be predicted with confidence. But some back-of-the-envelope calculations suggest that the world cannot afford to allow cropland to continue to slip away. If growth in grain yields increased by 1 percent per year (roughly the rate of growth in this decade), and if consumption per person remained at the 1995 level, more than 750 million hectares would be needed for grain by 2030. This area is 8 percent above the 1996 level, and 2.5 percent above the 1981 peak in grain area. While yields may be re-energized in the future, yield growth could well be offset by rising consumption per person as Asian economies continue to surge, and as the former Soviet republics emerge from their depression. Similar calculations for oilseeds, fruits and vegetables, and beverage crops all show increases in area needed.[72]

These quick calculations suggest a need for all of the idle European land, all of the sustainably cultivable U.S. Conservation Reserve Program land, and nearly all of the "reserve" land identified by the FAO (assuming it is actually available). In the face of such great need, continuing losses of quality cropland are unacceptably large.

Land for the Next Generation

Clearly, the global food production system will be seriously challenged in coming decades to feed a continually growing, increasingly affluent global population. Every hectare of sustainably croppable land that is lost means more pressure on yields to compensate for lost production. But if existing, sustainably farmed cropland is seen as a strategic resource, no less important to a nation's well-being than oil reserves or a national army, preservation can become a relatively straightforward matter.

In several European countries, agricultural land is already given the high levels of protection afforded to a strategic asset. In the United Kingdom, for example, permission is needed to develop agricultural land. Most development of rural land is presumed to damage the quality of open countryside, making it ineligible for development permits. By giving planning agencies in other countries a mandate to protect farmland and the authority to do so, losses could be sharply curtailed. [73]

Even where land is more freely developed, as in the United States, cropland losses could be reduced by requiring greater density in urban and suburban building. In the agriculture-rich Central Valley of California, for example, where population is expected to triple by 2040, cropland losses could be cut by an estimated 55 percent in that period simply by building 15 residential units per hectare, rather than the more typical 7 units. A denser urban environment also facilitates the use of sustainable transportation systems, saves money on infrastructure of many kinds, and can promote a greater sense of community.[74]

One way to encourage denser patterns of development is to use zoning authority to establish strict city limits that prevent urban encroachment on outlying agricultural areas. Adjacent to some cities in the United Kingdom, for example, a "greenbelt" of several miles' width is established on which development is virtually prohibited for long periods. In addition to saving farmland, the greenbelts separate neighboring cities, preserve rural landscapes, and avoid the problems that accompany the suburban sprawl found in many parts of the United States.[75]

In the absence of strong regulation of farmland use, control of cropland losses is more difficult. Voluntary arrangements that rely on financial incentives, such as the purchase of development rights from land owners, have shown modest success in preserving land. Under these arrangements—also known as conservation easements—a farmer agrees not to develop cropland for non-farm purposes in return for tax benefits or a cash payment. Where easements are perpetual, subsequent owners of the farm are also bound by the development restriction, and the land will remain in agricultural production permanently. In the United States, 169,000 hectares of farmland in 16 states have been preserved since 1976 through the purchase of development rights. With greater funding, the total could be much higher: according to the American Farmland Trust, funding in seven states was sufficient to preserve only 15 percent of the area that farmers wanted to place under protection.

Even with greater funding, however, the potential land savings are modest: more cropland is lost in the United States in two years than would have been saved in 20 years of conservation easement purchases, even assuming full program funding.[76]

Fiscal tools can also be enlisted to help preserve cropland. Where property and estate taxes work against such preservation, re-writing the tax laws would help. In some areas, farmers near cities are forced to sell their land to pay the rising property taxes that result when it becomes attractive to developers. Taxing farmland at its agricultural value, rather than its development value, would allow farmers to pay lower property taxes. With the costs of farming thus lowered, farmers would find it more profitable to remain on the land. Similarly, burdensome estate taxes are often attached to inherited land, and frequently force recipients to sell or subdivide their new holdings to pay estate taxes. Restructuring estate taxes to preserve farmland would help avoid the unwanted loss of land. This is especially necessary in countries where the farming population is aging. In the United States, for example, nearly half of farmers in Pennsylvania are 55 or older; much of the land they farm will change hands in the next two decades as current owners retire or die.[77]

One potentially powerful fiscal tool that has not been widely employed is a stiff farmland conversion tax. Heavily taxing the development of cropland would give owners a strong disincentive to take their land out of farming, but they would still maintain the freedom to do so. A farmland conversion tax would alter the dynamics of land markets and land use in countries that currently allow great latitude in the purchase and use of land.

Preservation of farmland, however, is no more than a delaying action unless measures are taken to protect soils as well. A number of initiatives are available to reduce the high levels of degradation that continue to rob soils of fertility, and to pull them from production. First, governments should provide incentives to farmers to remove from cultivation land that cannot be farmed sustainably. The United States, for example, has had great success with its Conservation Reserve Program (CRP), which pays farmers to retire marginal lands under ten-year contracts. On the half of CRP land that is highly erodible, sheet and rill erosion fell from 8.6 tons per hectare per year to 0.6 tons between 1982 and 1992. In all, more than 60 percent of the soil savings on cropland in the United States since 1985 are credited to this program.[78]

Governments can also play a constructive role by promoting the use of soil-conserving methods of production. Conservation tillage, terracing, alternative cropping arrangements, use of shelterbelts, and other soil-saving initiatives can be promoted through extension services, agricultural research agencies, non-governmental organizations, and other institutions with a presence in the field. In the United States, conservation tillage—a plowing technique that avoids wholesale overturning of the soil—was used on more than a third of U.S. cropland in 1994. Conservation practices of all kinds contributed to a 25 percent reduction in soil erosion in the United States between 1982 and 1992.[79]

In some areas, soils can be conserved by eliminating the conditions that force farmers to use them unsustainably. Poor farmers who till marginal hillside or forest land are often cultivating the only land available to them. The damage done to their soils can in many cases be avoided by allowing them to farm land that is underused. In some parts of Latin America, more equitable land distribution would likely stimulate more intensive use of farmland by putting into cultivation land that is now underutilized or lying idle.

To the extent that existing cropland is used more efficiently, pressure on cropland can be reduced. Agricultural research will need to focus on methods of production that are fruitful, environmentally benign, and adoptable by poor farmers on small plots of poor-quality land. Fortunately, alternative models of intensive agricultural production

already exist. One, known as bio-intensive farming, empha-
sizes nurturing of soils as a prerequisite for intensive and
sustainable production. Developed by agricultural
researcher John Jeavons, the approach uses carefully prepared soils to raise copious quantities of produce and grains
on small, nearly garden-size plots. Jeavons' reported suc-
cesses are impressive: yields greater than the commercial
average, from rocky hillside soil, using little water and no
chemical fertilizer. In addition to saving land *and* increasing
soil health, the approach is labor-
intensive, making it especially
appealing for developing countries,
where labor is plentiful. More institutional support and greater research
funding would help promising non-
traditional technologies like bio-
intensive farming to achieve their
full potential.[80]

Cropland is a strategic resource, no less important than oil reserves or a national army.

Pressure on agricultural land
can also be minimized by reducing
demand. Slowing the rate of population growth is the single most effective way to achieve large-scale reductions in
the demand for food, and to slow the shrinkage in cropland
per person. In a land-tight world, policies proven effective
in reducing population growth, such as quality education
for girls, economic security for women, and access to family
planning strategies have a direct impact on the extent and
use of cropland. As governments think strategically about
the agricultural land base, population policy cannot be
ignored.

Demand can also be reduced by using existing production more efficiently. More than 20 percent of harvested
food never makes it to the dinner table because of spoilage,
spillage, and losses to rodents and insects. Cutting these
losses would increase the supply of food without cultivating
more land or using it more intensively. A recently developed, tent-sized synthetic bag for storing sacks of harvested
grain is an example of the kind of advances needed. Once

zipped, the virtually airtight bag suffocates insects while keeping rodents out. The bag can also increase income: in field tests, Sri Lankan farmers stored their produce in the bag until after the harvest-time glut of grain, and saw incomes climb 30 percent.[81]

Perhaps the greatest potential for increasing food-use efficiency lies in reducing consumption of meat, a grain-intensive food. Roughly 2 of every 5 tons of grain produced in the world is fed to livestock, poultry, or fish; reducing consumption of these products, especially of beef, could free up massive quantities of grain and reduce pressures on land. Indeed, the most prosperous nations have plenty of room to reduce their meat (and therefore grain) consumption. Average annual grain consumption is just over 300 kilos per person globally, yet citizens of 18 nations consume well over 500 kilos, and the average American consumes more than 800 kilos. If the greatest consumers of grain had eaten 400 kilos of grain in 1995—the Italian level—grain production last year would have effectively increased by some 13 percent. This grain savings represents more than 70 million hectares of land. [82]

The need to protect the extent and quality of cropland is no less urgent today than it was for the ancient Sumerians. Once we recognize farmland as the base of our civilization as well as our food supply, measures to preserve land become easy to identify and implement. But in an increasingly crowded world, there is little time to waste in protecting our agricultural patrimony.

Notes

1. Clive Ponting, "Historical Perspectives on Sustainable Development," *Environment*, November 1990.

2. Lester R. Brown et al., *Vital Signs 1996: The Trends that are Shaping Our Future* (New York: W.W. Norton, 1996).

3. United States Department of Agriculture (USDA), Production, Supply, and Distribution (PS&D) (electronic database) (Washington, D.C., May 10, 1996). Grain self-sufficiency is measured as the ratio of production of total grains to consumption of total grains, 1969-71 average and 1993-95 average.

4. China from George P. Brown, "Arable Land Loss in Rural China," in *Asian Survey*, October 1995; U.S. from Natural Resources Conservation Service, *Summary Report: 1992 National Resources Inventory* (Washington, D.C.: USDA, January 1995).

5. USDA, PS&D, op. cit. note 3.

6. Carl Zoerb, "The Virgin Land Territory: Plans, Performance, Prospects," in Roy D. Laird, ed., *Soviet Agriculture: The Permanent Crisis* (New York: Praeger, 1965). Yield share is a Worldwatch calculation based on data in Lester Brown et al., *Vital Signs 1995: The Trends that are Shaping Our Future*, (New York: W.W. Norton, 1995), and Brown et al., op. cit. note 2.

7. Grain price decreases from International Monetary Fund (IMF), *International Financial Statistics Yearbook* (Washington, D.C., 1994), and IMF, *International Financial Statistics* (Washington, D.C.: May 1996); price changes were: rice, down 36%; wheat, down 13%; corn, down 16%; grain price increases from IMF, May 1996, op. cit. this note; price comparison is for first quarter 1995 and first quarter 1996: wheat was up 34%, corn 52%, and rice 32%.

8. Yield trends from USDA, PS&D, op. cit. note 3.

9. Grain harvested area from USDA PS&D, op. cit. note 3; population from Francis Urban and Ray Nightingale, "World Population by Country and Region, 1950-90 and Projections to 2050" (Washington, D.C.: Economic Research Service, USDA, April 1993); one hectare (ha) is equivalent in area to 1.39 soccer fields; 0.12 is roughly equal to 16.7% (one-sixth) of a soccer field.

10. Falling reserves from Lester R. Brown et al, op. cit. note 2; grain consumption from USDA PS&D, op. cit. note 3.

11. Department of Economic and Social Information and Policy Analysis, United Nations, *World Urbanization Prospects: the 1992 Revision* (New York, 1993); fastest urban expansion from Eugene Linden, "The Exploding Cities of the Developing World," *Foreign Affairs*, January/February 1996.

12. Dipasis Bhadra and Antonio Salazar P. Brandao, "Urbanization, Agricultural Development, and Land Allocation," World Bank Discussion Paper 201 (Washington, D.C.: World Bank, 1993).

13. Asian growth from IMF, *World Economic Outlook May 1996*, (Washington, 1996).

14. USDA estimate from Scott Thompson, "The Evolving Grain Markets in Southeast Asia," in *Grain: World Markets and Trade* (Washington, D.C.: USDA, Foreign Agricultural Service, June 1995); Java population, office space, and housing from Tommy Firman and Ida Ayu Indira Dharmapatni, "The Challenges to Sustainable Development in Jakarta Metropolitan Region," *Habitat International*, vol. 18, no. 3.

15. Projected loss is Worldwatch calculation based on data in Food and Agriculture Organization (FAO) *Production Yearbook 1994* (Rome, 1994); population estimate from Urban and Nightingale, op. cit. note 9; Prime Minister from "Development vs. Agriculture in Battle over Vietnam's Land," *Earth Island Journal*, Winter 1995-96.

16. Brown, op. cit. note 4. Arable land in China is officially listed as 96 million ha, but this is widely acknowledged to be understated. Estimates of actual cropped area range from 123 million ha to as high as 150 million. Following the work of Vaclav Smil, this paper assumes cropland area to be 130 million ha. See Smil, "Environmental Problems in China: Estimates of Economic Costs" (Honolulu: East-West Center, April 1996).

17. Current underreporting from Brown, op. cit. note 4; earlier estimates of land loss from Shujie Yao, *Agricultural reform and grain prices in China* (London: St. Martin's Press, 1994), who reported losses of 500,000 ha (net) per year, or 1.33 million ha (gross) between 1952 and the late 1970s; World Bank, *China: Agriculture to the Year 2000* (Washington, 1985), which reported losses of about a million ha per year to non-agricultural uses between 1959 and 1978; and Vaclav Smil, op. cit. note 16, who reports gross losses of nearly 30 million ha between 1957 and 1977 (1.5 million ha per year).

18. Smil, op. cit. note 16.

19. Brown, op. cit. note 4. The share of China's land is a Worldwatch calculation that assumes total cropped area of 130 million ha.

20. Natural Resources Conservation Service, op. cit. note 4; American Farmland Trust (AFT), "Farming on the Edge" (Washington, D.C., June 1994); USDA, "U.S. Agricultural Exports and Imports," *Agricultural Outlook*,

May 1996.

21. AFT, "Alternatives for Future Urban Growth in California's Central Valley: The Bottom Line for Agriculture and Taxpayers" (Washington, D.C., October 1995); California loss estimate from Department of Conservation, State of California, *Farmland Conversion Report* (Sacramento, various years); L.A. County from Valerie Berton, "Harvest or Homes? AFT Research Highlights Need to Protect Ag as Central Valley Grows," *American Farmland* (Washington, D.C.: AFT, Fall 1995).

22. China from Odil Tunali, "A Billion Cars: The Road Ahead," *World Watch*, January/February 1996; Vietnam from Jeremy Grant, "Vietnam Trebles Car Import Quota," *Financial Times*, January 12, 1996.

23. Road estimates based on data in International Road Federation, *World Road Statistics 1989-1993* (Washington, D.C., 1994) and American Automobile Manufacturers Association, *World Motor Vehicle Data* (Washington, D.C., 1995).

24. Thailand from James Fahn, "Fore!" *The Nation*, January 14, 1994, and Anita Pleumarom, "Course and Effect," *The Ecologist*, May/June 1992; Japan from Philip Shenon, "FORE! Golf in Asia Hits Environmental Rough," *New York Times*, October 22, 1994.

25. Analysis modeled on that found in Pierre Crosson and Jock Anderson, "Resources and Global Food Prospects: Supply and Demand for Cereals to 2030," World Bank Technical Paper Number 184 (Washington: World Bank, 1992). Land use patterns vary greatly from city to city; the 0.05 ha estimate is at best very rough. Urban population figures from United Nations, *World Demographic Estimates and Projections, 1950-2025* (New York, 1988).

26. Ashali Varma, "Target: 600 New Cities by the Year 2010," *The Earth Times*, April 15-30, 1996; population increase from Urban and Nightingale, op. cit. note 9.

27. Worldwatch calculation, based on data in Department of Conservation, op. cit. note 21, and Natural Resources Conservation Service, op. cit. note 4.

28. Irrigation's share of world food from Sandra Postel, "Forging a Sustainable Water Strategy," *State of the World 1996* (New York: W.W. Norton, 1996); irrigation's share of past output from Pierre Crosson, "Future Supplies of Land and Water for World Agriculture," revision of a paper presented at a conference of the International Food Policy Research Institute (IFPRI) in February 1994 (Washington: Resources for the Future, August 1994).

29. The *FAO Production Yearbook 1994* (Rome, 1994) shows a decline in global irrigated area for 1992-93 of 0.6 percent.   Irrigated area for

Kazakhstan, Kyrgyzstan, Tajikistan, Turkmenistan, and Uzbekistan, however, which is registered as declining in the FAO yearbooks, is reported by the World Bank to have increased between 1990 and 1994. If FAO data is adjusted using the World Bank data, global irrigated area shows a slight decline of 0.2 percent. Deceleration in irrigation growth from FAO, *State of Food and Agriculture 1993* (Rome, 1993).

30. Yuri Markish, Agriculture and Trade Analysis Division, Economic Research Service, USDA, personal communication, June 4, 1996.

31. Department of Conservation, State of California, *Farmland Conversion Report, 1990-92* (Sacramento, June 1994).

32. Area affected by overpumping is a Worldwatch estimate based on data in the following: Libya from World Resources Institute et al., *World Resources: A Guide to the Global Environment 1996-97* (Oxford: Oxford University Press, 1996); Arabian Peninsula from Jamil al Alawi and Mohammed Abdulrazzak, "Water in the Arabian Peninsula: Problems and Perspectives," in Peter Rogers and Peter Lydon, *Water in the Arab World* (Cambridge, MA: Division of Applied Sciences, Harvard University, 1994); California from Pacific Institute, *California Water 2020: A Sustainable Vision* (Oakland, CA: Pacific Institute for Studies in Development, Environment, and Security, 1995); High Plains from Allan Burns, United States Geological Survey, personal communication, June 18, 1996, and U.S. Geological Survey, "Water-Level Changes in the High Plains Aquifer, Predevelopment to 1994," at Web address http://h2o.usgs.gov/public/wid/FS_215-95/FS_215-95.html; North China from Ye Yongyi, "Policies for Sustainable Water Resources Development in the North China Region," in United Nations, Economic and Social Commission for Asia and the Pacific, *Towards an Environmentally Sound and Sustainable Development of Water Resources in Asia and the Pacific*, Water Resources Series no. 71 (Bangkok, 1992), and Xu Zhifang, unpublished paper prepared for the World Water Council—Interim Founding Committee, March 1995; India from B.H. Dhawan, "Magnitude of Groundwater Exploitation," *Economic and Political Weekly*, April 8, 1995, and S.P. Sharma, Ministry of Agriculture, Government of India, personal communication, June 17, 1996; Iran from United Nations Development Programme (UNDP), *Land Degradation in South Asia: Its Severity, Causes, and Effects Upon the People*, World Soil Resources Reports 78 (Nairobi, 1994).

33. Arabian Peninsula from al Alawi and Abdulrazzak, op. cit. note 32.

34. J.T. Musick, F.B. Pringle, W.L. Harman, and B.A. Stewart, "Long-Term Irrigation Trends—Texas High Plains," *Applied Engineering in Agriculture*, November 1990.

35. World Bank, *Rapid Urban Environmental Assessment: Lessons from Cities in the Developing World*, vol. 1, (Washington, D.C., 1994); Ren Guanzhao, "Urban Water Supply in China," in United Nations, Economic and Social

Commission for Asia and the Pacific, *Urban Water Resources Management,* Water Resources Series no. 72 (New York, 1993); Patrick Tyler, "China's Fickle Rivers: Dry Farms, Needy Industry Bring a Water Crisis," *New York Times,* May 23, 1996.

36. The reduction was likely greater than 25 percent. See Steve van Beek, *The Chao Phya: River in Transition* (Oxford: Oxford University Press, 1995). Share of Thai harvested area from USDA PS&D, op. cit. note 3.

37. Dennis Rule, Tucson Water Department, Tucson, AZ, personal communication, April 29, 1996; Gary Bostrom, Water Resources Department, Colorado Springs, CO, personal communication, April 29, 1996; Penn Loh and Anna Steding, "The Palo Verde Test Land Fallowing Program: A Model for Future California Water Transfers?" (Oakland, CA: Pacific Institute for Studies in Development, Environment, and Security, March 1996).

38. Ministry of the Environment, *The Environment in Israel* (Jerusalem, 1992), and "The Environment in Israel," *Israel Environment Bulletin* Spring-Summer 1994; India from Marcus Moench, "Approaches to Groundwater Management: To Control or Enable?" *Economic and Political Weekly,* September 24, 1994; China from Smil, op. cit. note 16.

39. Worldwatch calculation based on population data from Urban and Nightingale, op. cit. note 9, and from Fred Pearce, "High and Dry in Aswan, *New Scientist,* July 7, 1994. Pearce reports that the average flow of the Nile in the 1980s was 76 billion cubic meters. Nile flow is commonly cited as 84 billion cubic meters.

40. Operations Evaluation Department, "A Review of World Bank Experience in Irrigation" (Washington: World Bank, November 3, 1994).

41. Robert Goodland, "Environmental Sustainability Needs Renewable Energy: The Extent to Which Big Hydro is Part of the Transition," paper presented to the International Crane Foundation Workshop, Washington, D.C., November 28–December 2, 1995.

42. Paul Raskin, Evan Hansen, and Robert Margolis, *Water and Sustainability: A Global Outlook,* Polestar Series Report No. 4 (Stockholm: Stockholm Environment Institute, 1995).

43. United Nations study is L.R. Oldeman et al., *World Map of the Status of Human-Induced Soil Degradation: An Explanatory Note,* 2nd ed. (Wageningen, Netherlands, and Nairobi: International Soil Reference and Information Centre and United Nations Environment Programme, 1991); study of Asia is Anthony Young, *Land Degradation in South Asia: Its Severity, Causes, and Effects upon the People,* World Soil Resources Reports 78 (Rome: FAO, 1994).

44. Strong and extreme degradation from L.R. Oldeman, personal communication, September 21, 1995; production capacity of lost area is a

Worldwatch calculation that assumes a modest yield of 3 tons per hectare, and that 1 ton will feed three people; today's losses from Sara J. Scherr and Satya Yadav, "Land Degradation in the Developing World: Implications for Food, Agriculture, and the Environment to 2020," Food, Agriculture, and the Environment Discussion Paper 14 (Washington: IFPRI, May 1996), and Oldeman, op. cit. note 43.

45. Worldwatch calculation based on a methodology suggested in Pierre Crosson, "Soil Erosion and Its On-Farm Productivity Consequences: What Do We Know?" Discussion Paper 95-29 (Washington, D.C.: Resources for the Future, June 1995), and on Oldeman, op. cit. note 44.

46. Oldeman, op. cit. note 43; net and gross erosion from Crosson, op. cit. note 45.

47. China from Vaclav Smil, "Environmental Problems in China: Estimates of Economic Costs" (Honolulu: East-West Center, April 1996), and Jikun Huang and Scott Rozelle, "Environmental Stress and Grain Yields in China," *American Journal of Agricultural Economics*, November 1995; Russia from Sergei Bobyliev and Bo Libert, "Prospects for Agricultural and Environmental Policy Integration in Russia," *Agriculture and the Environment in the Transition to a Market Economy* (Paris: Organisation for Economic Co-operation and Development (OECD), 1994); Iran from Young, op.cit. note 43; Pakistan from H. E. Dregne, "Erosion and Soil Productivity in Asia," *Journal of Soil and Water Conservation*, January-February 1992, and Young, op. cit. note 43; Haiti from Thomas A. White and Jon L. Jickling, "An Economic and Institutional Analysis of Soil Conservation in Haiti," in Ernst Lutz, Stefano Pagiola, and Carlos Reiche, eds., *Economic and Institutional Analyses of Soil Conservation Projects in Central America and the Caribbean*, World Bank Environment Paper Number 8 (Washington, D.C., 1994); Australia from F. Ghassemi, A.J. Jakeman, and H.A. Nix, *Salinisation of Land and Water Resources: Human Causes, Extent, Management, and Case Studies* (Wallingford, Oxon, UK: CAB International, 1995), and Arthur and Jeanette Conacher, *Rural Land Degradation in Australia* (Oxford: Oxford University Press, 1995).

48. Oldeman, op. cit. note 43.

49. 160 million ha from Per Pinstrup Andersen and Rajul Pandya-Lorch, "Alleviating Poverty, Intensifying Agriculture, and Effectively Managing Natural Resources," Food, Agriculture, and the Environment Discussion Paper 1 (Washington, D.C.: Food Policy Research Institute, 1994); Philippines from Maria Concepcion Cruz et al., "Population Growth, Poverty, and Environmental Stress: Frontier Migration in the Philippines and Costa Rica" (Washington, D.C.: World Resources Institute, 1992).

50. Miguel A. Altieri, *Agroecology: The Scientific Basis of Alternative Agriculture* (Boulder: Westview Special Studies in Agriculture, Science, and Policy); Africa and Southeast Asia from Joy Tivy, *Agricultural Ecology* (Essex, UK:

Longman Scientific and Technical, 1990).

51. "Low-potential" lands from Andersen and Pandya-Lorch, op. cit. note 49; shifting cultivation from N.C. Brady, "Making Agriculture a Sustainable Industry," in Clive A. Edwards et al., *Sustainable Agricultural Systems* (Ankeny, Iowa: Soil and Water Conservation Society, 1990).

52. Sandra Postel, *State of the World 1996* (New York: W.W. Norton, 1996); Central Asia yields from FAO, *State of Food and Agriculture 1995* (Rome, 1995).

53. Worldwatch calculation based on land loss data in Oldeman, op. cit. note 43.

54. Calculated from data in FAO, *FAO Production Yearbook*, (Rome, various years).

55. Grainland area decline from USDA, PS&D, op. cit. note 3; other foods from FAO, op. cit. note 54; Figure 3 from FAO, *FAO Production Yearbook* (Rome, various years), and from USDA, op. cit. note 3.

56. USDA, PS&D, op. cit. note 3. World grain yields increased by 79 percent between 1964 and 1994, while soybean yields increased by 63 percent.

57. Meal share of soybeans from USDA, "Oilseeds: World Markets and Trade" (Washington, D.C.: Foreign Agricultural Service, USDA, October 1995); grain to livestock from Lester R. Brown, "World Feedgrain Use Drops," in Lester R. Brown et al., *Vital Signs 1996* (New York: W.W. Norton, 1996).

58. Fruits and vegetables from FAO, op cit. 54; China based on data in Lester R. Brown, *Who Will Feed China?* (New York: W.W. Norton, 1995).

59. Area increases from FAO, op. cit. note 52; industrial crops from Lewrene Glaser, Charles Plummer, and Donald Van Dyne, "Industry Expands Use of Agricultural Commodities," *Agricultural Outlook*, January-February 1996.

60. Projection made using population data from Urban and Nightingale, op. cit. note 9.

61. Contracting Kazakh area from USDA, PS&D, op. cit note 3, and FAO, op. cit. note 52.

62. CRP area from Natural Resources Conservation Service, op. cit. note 4; Everglades from John H. Cushman, "Clinton Backing Vast Effort to Restore Florida Swamps," *New York Times*, February 18, 1996, and Elizabeth Levitan Spaid and Kirk Nielsen, "Florida Cane Farmers Sour on Everglades Restoration," *Christian Science Monitor*, February 21, 1996.

63. George P. Brown, op. cit. note 4.

64. Roughly half of the CRP land is classified as "highly erodible cultivated cropland." This paper assumes that the rest, some 7 million ha, is sustainably cultivable, using careful practices. See USDA, "1992 National Resources Inventory—Highlights," information sheet (Washington, D.C., July 13, 1994). The U.S. General Accounting Office (GAO) estimates that buffer strips covering 2.5 million ha—one-sixth the size of the current CRP land—could provide a minimum level of environmental protection, which would release a greater amount of CRP land for farming. It acknowledges, however, that environmental goals such as wildlife protection would not be met through a buffer strip program. See GAO, "Conservation Reserve Program: Alternatives are Available for Managing Environmentally Sensitive Cropland," Report to the Committee on Agriculture, Nutrition, and Forestry, U.S. Senate (Washington, D.C., February 1995). European set-aside grain area of approximately 4 million ha calculated from data in USDA, "Grain: World Markets and Trade," Foreign Agricultural Service, Circular Series FG 6-96 (Washington, D.C., June 1996).

65. Nikos Alexandratos, ed., *World Agriculture: Towards 2010* (Rome: FAO, 1995).

66. Nigel Smith, *Rainforest Corridors: The TransAmazon Colonization Scheme* (Berkeley: University of California Press, 1982); Douglas Ian Stewart, *After the Trees: Living on the Transamazon Highway* (Austin: University of Texas Press, 1994); Bruce Babbitt, "Amazon Grace," *The New Republic*, June 25, 1990.

67. Junus Kartasubrata, "Indonesia," in *Sustainable Agriculture and the Environment in the Humid Tropics* (Washington, D.C.: National Academy Press, 1993).

68. Virginia H. Dale, Richard A. Houghton, Alan Grainger, Ariel E. Lugo, and Sandra Brown, "Emissions of Greenhouse Gases from Tropical Deforestation and Subsequent Uses of the Land," in National Research Council, *Sustainable Agriculture and the Environment in the Humid Tropics* (Washington, D.C.: National Academy of Sciences, 1993).

69. Alexandratos, op. cit. note 65.

70. FAO, *Report on the 1980 World Census of Agriculture,* Census Bulletin No. 22 (Rome, April 1986).

71. Lester R. Brown and Hal Kane, *Full House: Reassessing the Earth's Population Carrying Capacity* (New York: W.W. Norton).

72. Worldwatch calculation based on data in USDA, PS&D, op. cit. note 3. Other calculations are as follows: Oilseeds—If global oilseed yields rise as they have over the past 15 years, and if per capita consumption rises only half as fast as it did in that period, roughly 40 million ha of harvested area—an area the size of Paraguay—will be needed by 2010 to meet the additional demand. Luxury and Non-food Crops—If the area dedicated to sugar, coffee, cocoa, tea, and hops (luxury crops) rises at the same rate to 2010 as it has since 1980, another 7 million ha will be needed. For non-food crops, the equivalent calculation results in more than 5 million ha required.

73. European policies from Margaret Rosso Grossman and Wim Brussaard, eds., *Agrarian Land Law in the Western World* (Wallingford, UK: CAB International, 1992); UK from William Howarth and Christopher P. Rodgers, eds., *Agriculture, Conservation and Land Use* (Cardiff: University of Wales Press, 1993).

74. AFT, "Alternatives for Future Urban Growth in California's Central Valley: The Bottom Line for Agriculture and Taxpayers" (Washington: AFT, October 1995).

75. Howarth and Rodgers, op. cit. note 73.

76. Charles Beretz, AFT, Washington, D.C., personal communication, June 13, 1996, and Jennifer Dempsey, AFT, Northampton, MA, personal communication, June 12, 1996.

77. "AFT Joins Pennsylvania Farm Link Effort," *American Farmland*, Spring 1996.

78. USDA, "1992 National Resources Inventory: Highlights," Soil Conservation Service, July 13, 1994.

79. Conservation tillage use from Conservation Technology Information Center (CTIC), "1994 National Crop Residue Management Survey, Executive Summary" (West Lafayette, IN, 1994); reduction in erosion from Natural Resources Conservation Service, op. cit. note 4.

80. Dr. William Liebhardt, University of California at Davis, personal communication, May 20, 1996; "Intensive Micro-Farming May Help Fill Tables in Third World," *Christian Science Monitor*, October 16, 1987.

81. Waste rate from Margaret Biswas, "Agriculture and Environment: A Review, 1972–1992," *Ambio*, May 1994; grainbag from Joseph Axelrod, GrainPro, Inc., Boston, MA, private communication, July 31, 1995.

82. Share of grain to livestock from Lester R. Brown et al., op. cit. note 20.

PUBLICATION ORDER FORM

No. of
Copies

_____ 65. **Reversing Africa's Decline** by Lester R. Brown and Edward C. Wolf.
_____ 66. **World Oil: Coping With the Dangers of Success** by Christopher Flavin.
_____ 68. **Banishing Tobacco** by William U. Chandler.
_____ 70. **Electricity For A Developing World: New Directions** by Christopher Flavin.
_____ 75. **Reassessing Nuclear Power: The Fallout From Chernobyl** by Christopher Flavin.
_____ 77. **The Future of Urbanization: Facing the Ecological and Economic Constraints**
         by Lester R. Brown and Jodi L. Jacobson.
_____ 78. **On the Brink of Extinction: Conserving The Diversity of Life** by Edward C. Wolf.
_____ 79. **Defusing the Toxics Threat: Controlling Pesticides and Industrial Waste**
         by Sandra Postel.
_____ 80. **Planning the Global Family** by Jodi L. Jacobson.
_____ 81. **Renewable Energy: Today's Contribution, Tomorrow's Promise** by
         Cynthia Pollock Shea.
_____ 82. **Building on Success: The Age of Energy Efficiency** by Christopher Flavin
         and Alan B. Durning.
_____ 84. **Rethinking the Role of the Automobile** by Michael Renner.
_____ 86. **Environmental Refugees: A Yardstick of Habitability** by Jodi L. Jacobson.
_____ 89. **National Security: The Economic and Environmental Dimensions** by Michael Renner.
_____ 90. **The Bicycle: Vehicle for a Small Planet** by Marcia D. Lowe.
_____ 91. **Slowing Global Warming: A Worldwide Strategy** by Christopher Flavin
_____ 92. **Poverty and the Environment: Reversing the Downward Spiral** by Alan B. Durning.
_____ 93. **Water for Agriculture: Facing the Limits** by Sandra Postel.
_____ 94. **Clearing the Air: A Global Agenda** by Hilary F. French.
_____ 95. **Apartheid's Environmental Toll** by Alan B. Durning.
_____ 96. **Swords Into Plowshares: Converting to a Peace Economy** by Michael Renner.
_____ 97. **The Global Politics of Abortion** by Jodi L. Jacobson.
_____ 98. **Alternatives to the Automobile: Transport for Livable Cities** by Marcia D. Lowe.
_____ 99. **Green Revolutions: Environmental Reconstruction in Eastern Europe and the**
         Soviet Union by Hilary F. French.
_____ 100. **Beyond the Petroleum Age: Designing a Solar Economy** by Christopher Flavin
         and Nicholas Lenssen.
_____ 101. **Discarding the Throwaway Society** by John E. Young.
_____ 102. **Women's Reproductive Health: The Silent Emergency** by Jodi L. Jacobson.
_____ 103. **Taking Stock: Animal Farming and the Environment** by Alan B. Durning and
         Holly B. Brough.
_____ 104. **Jobs in a Sustainable Economy** by Michael Renner.
_____ 105. **Shaping Cities: The Environmental and Human Dimensions** by Marcia D. Lowe.
_____ 106. **Nuclear Waste: The Problem That Won't Go Away** by Nicholas Lenssen.
_____ 107. **After the Earth Summit: The Future of Environmental Governance**
         by Hilary F. French.
_____ 108. **Life Support: Conserving Biological Diversity** by John C. Ryan.
_____ 109. **Mining the Earth** by John E. Young.
_____ 110. **Gender Bias: Roadblock to Sustainable Development** by Jodi L. Jacobson.
_____ 111. **Empowering Development: The New Energy Equation** by Nicholas Lenssen.
_____ 112. **Guardians of the Land: Indigenous Peoples and the Health of the Earth**
         by Alan Thein Durning.
_____ 113. **Costly Tradeoffs: Reconciling Trade and the Environment** by Hilary F. French.
_____ 114. **Critical Juncture: The Future of Peacekeeping** by Michael Renner.
_____ 115. **Global Network: Computers in a Sustainable Society** by John E. Young.
_____ 116. **Abandoned Seas: Reversing the Decline of the Oceans** by Peter Weber.
_____ 117. **Saving the Forests: What Will It Take?** by Alan Thein Durning.
_____ 118. **Back on Track: The Global Rail Revival** by Marcia D. Lowe.
_____ 119. **Powering the Future: Blueprint for a Sustainable Electricity Industry**
         by Christopher Flavin and Nicholas Lenssen.
_____ 120. **Net Loss: Fish, Jobs, and the Marine Environment** by Peter Weber.

_____121. **The Next Efficiency Revolution: Creating a Sustainable Materials Economy** by John E. Young and Aaron Sachs.

_____122. **Budgeting for Disarmament: The Costs of War and Peace** by Michael Renner.

_____123. **High Priorities: Conserving Mountain Ecosystems and Cultures** by Derek Denniston.

_____124. **A Building Revolution: How Ecology and Health Concerns Are Transforming Construction** by David Malin Roodman and Nicholas Lenssen.

_____125. **The Hour of Departure: Forces That Create Refugees and Migrants** by Hal Kane.

_____126. **Partnership for the Planet: An Environmental Agenda for the United Nations** by Hilary F. French.

—————127. **Eco-Justice: Linking Human Rights and the Environment** by Aaron Sachs.

_____128. **Imperiled Waters, Impoverished Future: The Decline of Freshwater Ecosystems** by Janet N. Abramovitz.

_____129. **Infecting Ourselves: How Environmental and Social Disruptions Trigger Disease** by Anne E. Platt.

_____130. **Climate of Hope: New Strategies for Stabilizing the World's Atmosphere** by Christopher Flavin and Odil Tunali.

_____131. **Shrinking Fields: Cropland Loss in a World of Eight Billion** by Gary Gardner

_____ **Total Copies**

Single Copy: $5.00   •   2–5: $4.00 ea.   •   6–20: $3.00 ea. •   21 or more: $2.00 ea.
Call Director of Communication at (202) 452-1999 to inquire about discounts on larger orders.

☐ **Membership in the Worldwatch Library: $30.00 (international airmail $45.00)**
The paperback edition of our 250-page "annual physical of the planet," *State of the World*, plus all Worldwatch Papers released during the calendar year.

☐ **Subscription to *World Watch* magazine: $20.00 (international airmail $35.00)**
Stay abreast of global environmental trends and issues with our award-winning, eminently readable bimonthly magazine.

☐ **Worldwatch Database Disk Subscription: One year for $89**
Includes current global agricultural, energy, economic, environmental, social, and military indicators from all current Worldwatch publications. Includes a mid-year update, and *Vital Signs* and *State of the World* as they are published. Can be used with Lotus 1-2-3, Quattro Pro, Excel, SuperCalc and many other spreadsheets.
Check one: _____high-density IBM-compatible or _____Macintosh

---

Make check payable to Worldwatch Institute
1776 Massachusetts Avenue, N.W., Washington, D.C. 20036-1904 USA

Please include $3 postage and handling for non-subscription orders.

Enclosed is my check for U.S. $_____
AMEX ☐ VISA ☐ Mastercard ☐ _____

<table>
<tr><td>Card Number</td><td>Expiration Date</td></tr>
</table>

_____

name   **daytime phone #**

_____

address

_____

city   **state**   **zip/country**
Phone: (202) 452-1999   Fax: (202) 296-7365   E-Mail: wwpub@worldwatch   WWP

____121. **The Next Efficiency Revolution: Creating a Sustainable Materials Economy** by John E. Young and Aaron Sachs.

____122. **Budgeting for Disarmament: The Costs of War and Peace** by Michael Renner.

____123. **High Priorities: Conserving Mountain Ecosystems and Cultures** by Derek Denniston.

____124. **A Building Revolution: How Ecology and Health Concerns Are Transforming Construction** by David Malin Roodman and Nicholas Lenssen.

____125. **The Hour of Departure: Forces That Create Refugees and Migrants** by Hal Kane.

____126. **Partnership for the Planet: An Environmental Agenda for the United Nations** by Hilary F. French.

————127. **Eco-Justice: Linking Human Rights and the Environment** by Aaron Sachs.

____128. **Imperiled Waters, Impoverished Future: The Decline of Freshwater Ecosystems** by Janet N. Abramovitz.

____129. **Infecting Ourselves: How Environmental and Social Disruptions Trigger Disease** by Anne E. Platt.

____130. **Climate of Hope: New Strategies for Stabilizing the World's Atmosphere** by Christopher Flavin and Odil Tunali.

____131. **Shrinking Fields: Cropland Loss in a World of Eight Billion** by Gary Gardner

_____ **Total Copies**

Single Copy: $5.00 • 2–5: $4.00 ea. • 6–20: $3.00 ea. • 21 or more: $2.00 ea.
Call Director of Communication at (202) 452-1999 to inquire about discounts on larger orders.

☐ **Membership in the Worldwatch Library: $30.00 (international airmail $45.00)**
The paperback edition of our 250-page "annual physical of the planet,"
State of the World, plus all Worldwatch Papers released during the calendar year.

☐ **Subscription to *World Watch* magazine: $20.00 (international airmail $35.00)**
Stay abreast of global environmental trends and issues with our award-winning, eminently readable bimonthly magazine.

☐ **Worldwatch Database Disk Subscription: One year for $89**
Includes current global agricultural, energy, economic, environmental, social, and military indicators from all current Worldwatch publications. Includes a mid-year update, and *Vital Signs* and *State of the World* as they are published. Can be used with Lotus 1-2-3, Quattro Pro, Excel, SuperCalc and many other spreadsheets.
Check one: _____high-density IBM-compatible or _____Macintosh

---

Make check payable to Worldwatch Institute
1776 Massachusetts Avenue, N.W., Washington, D.C. 20036-1904 USA

Please include $3 postage and handling for non-subscription orders.

Enclosed is my check for U.S. $_____
AMEX ☐ VISA ☐ Mastercard ☐ _____
                                    Card Number   Expiration Date

_____
name   **daytime phone #**

_____
address

_____
city   **state**   **zip/country**

Phone: (202) 452-1999   Fax: (202) 296-7365   E-Mail: wwpub@worldwatch   WWP

PUBLICATION ORDER FORM

No. of
Copies

_____ 65. **Reversing Africa's Decline** by Lester R. Brown and Edward C. Wolf.
_____ 66. **World Oil: Coping With the Dangers of Success** by Christopher Flavin.
_____ 68. **Banishing Tobacco** by William U. Chandler.
_____ 70. **Electricity For A Developing World: New Directions** by Christopher Flavin.
_____ 75. **Reassessing Nuclear Power: The Fallout From Chernobyl** by Christopher Flavin.
_____ 77. **The Future of Urbanization: Facing the Ecological and Economic Constraints** by Lester R. Brown and Jodi L. Jacobson.
_____ 78. **On the Brink of Extinction: Conserving The Diversity of Life** by Edward C. Wolf.
_____ 79. **Defusing the Toxics Threat: Controlling Pesticides and Industrial Waste** by Sandra Postel.
_____ 80. **Planning the Global Family** by Jodi L. Jacobson.
_____ 81. **Renewable Energy: Today's Contribution, Tomorrow's Promise** by Cynthia Pollock Shea.
_____ 82. **Building on Success: The Age of Energy Efficiency** by Christopher Flavin and Alan B. Durning.
_____ 84. **Rethinking the Role of the Automobile** by Michael Renner.
_____ 86. **Environmental Refugees: A Yardstick of Habitability** by Jodi L. Jacobson.
_____ 89. **National Security: The Economic and Environmental Dimensions** by Michael Renner.
_____ 90. **The Bicycle: Vehicle for a Small Planet** by Marcia D. Lowe.
_____ 91. **Slowing Global Warming: A Worldwide Strategy** by Christopher Flavin
_____ 92. **Poverty and the Environment: Reversing the Downward Spiral** by Alan B. Durning.
_____ 93. **Water for Agriculture: Facing the Limits** by Sandra Postel.
_____ 94. **Clearing the Air: A Global Agenda** by Hilary F. French.
_____ 95. **Apartheid's Environmental Toll** by Alan B. Durning.
_____ 96. **Swords Into Plowshares: Converting to a Peace Economy** by Michael Renner.
_____ 97. **The Global Politics of Abortion** by Jodi L. Jacobson.
_____ 98. **Alternatives to the Automobile: Transport for Livable Cities** by Marcia D. Lowe.
_____ 99. **Green Revolutions: Environmental Reconstruction in Eastern Europe and the Soviet Union** by Hilary F. French.
_____ 100. **Beyond the Petroleum Age: Designing a Solar Economy** by Christopher Flavin and Nicholas Lenssen.
_____ 101. **Discarding the Throwaway Society** by John E. Young.
_____ 102. **Women's Reproductive Health: The Silent Emergency** by Jodi L. Jacobson.
_____ 103. **Taking Stock: Animal Farming and the Environment** by Alan B. Durning and Holly B. Brough.
_____ 104. **Jobs in a Sustainable Economy** by Michael Renner.
_____ 105. **Shaping Cities: The Environmental and Human Dimensions** by Marcia D. Lowe.
_____ 106. **Nuclear Waste: The Problem That Won't Go Away** by Nicholas Lenssen.
_____ 107. **After the Earth Summit: The Future of Environmental Governance** by Hilary F. French.
_____ 108. **Life Support: Conserving Biological Diversity** by John C. Ryan.
_____ 109. **Mining the Earth** by John E. Young.
_____ 110. **Gender Bias: Roadblock to Sustainable Development** by Jodi L. Jacobson.
_____ 111. **Empowering Development: The New Energy Equation** by Nicholas Lenssen.
_____ 112. **Guardians of the Land: Indigenous Peoples and the Health of the Earth** by Alan Thein Durning.
_____ 113. **Costly Tradeoffs: Reconciling Trade and the Environment** by Hilary F. French.
_____ 114. **Critical Juncture: The Future of Peacekeeping** by Michael Renner.
_____ 115. **Global Network: Computers in a Sustainable Society** by John E. Young.
_____ 116. **Abandoned Seas: Reversing the Decline of the Oceans** by Peter Weber.
_____ 117. **Saving the Forests: What Will It Take?** by Alan Thein Durning.
_____ 118. **Back on Track: The Global Rail Revival** by Marcia D. Lowe.
_____ 119. **Powering the Future: Blueprint for a Sustainable Electricity Industry** by Christopher Flavin and Nicholas Lenssen.
_____ 120. **Net Loss: Fish, Jobs, and the Marine Environment** by Peter Weber.